Practical Theology in Action

Practical Theology in Action

Christian thinking in the service of Church and society

PAUL BALLARD
and
JOHN PRITCHARD

SPCK

First published in Great Britain in 1996

Society for Promoting Christian Knowledge
36 Causton Street
London SW1P 4ST

Second edition published 2006

British Library Cataloguing-in-Publication Data
A catalogue record for this book is available from the British Library

ISBN-13: 978–0–281–05719–1
ISBN-10: 0–281–05719–2

1 3 5 7 9 10 8 6 4 2

Typeset by Kenneth Burnley, Wirral, Cheshire
Printed in Great Britain by Ashford Colour Press

Contents

Preface to the First Edition

This book arose out of a response to a felt need. Practical theology, in its modern form, has now become an established part of the theological spectrum. The 1960s were the foundation years for the subject in its contemporary guise. That period of experimentation and the subsequent period of consolidation were summarized in 1986 by the publication of *The Foundations of Pastoral Studies and Practical Theology* (see Chapter 1), a series of essays produced by a working party of teachers that met for two years in Bristol. That laid down a marker and provided a point of reference. But time has not stood still and new developments have suggested that it is appropriate once more to reflect on where practical theology has come in ten years. In some ways the need remains the same: to provide a rationale and theological focus in a field that is increasingly diverse both in aim and content and in its institutionalized expressions. So the first task of the present book is to discuss the nature of practical theology as a theological discipline and to stress its importance as a theological activity in relation to other strands of theology. The other task, however, is to meet the lack of any basic introduction to the field. In this country, at least, there seems to be nothing for the novice who is setting out on to what can appear to be uncharted waters. Four groups of people were in mind.

First, every year, a considerable number of students embark on courses that include practical theology. Many of them, but by no means all, are training for the ordained ministry. Others will be there for any number of reasons, preparing for other ministries or simply wanting to root their theological learning in practice. These courses will be very differently packaged, ranging from

working in a traditional classroom to reflection on field experience, from a series of standard theological courses to practically
based learning or self-taught reading/tutorial courses. But for
most of them practical theology is a new field which is going to
make new demands. Such students could benefit from a resource
that offers an orientation and a way into the demands of the
subject.

The second group is the increasing number of lay people
involved in various forms of ministry and pastoral care, such as
ministry teams, lay pastors, Methodist Local Preachers, Anglican
Readers, pastoral auxiliaries and all those involved in the practical
action of the local church.

The third group in our minds are colleagues who take up
appointments in the subject. Some are likely to be moving from
practice in the field into a teaching situation. Their previous
educational experience may be many years ago, out of date or
formally academic. Others may be moving from a background of
training in other professional fields and need to learn about doing
theology. Others may be moving from theoretical theology to
the practical. For many, practical theology is, in any case, an
unknown quantity. It is hoped that an introduction such as this
will enable them to use their gifts and wisdom in a theologically
creative way.

The fourth group is more eclectic: those who for any reason
may be curious as to what practical theologians think they are
doing. This could include colleagues from other theological disciplines or church leaders interested in training issues, lay persons
just wanting to be informed, or those in other professions interested in how their colleagues in the Church tick.

This book sets out to do a number of things. Part I enquires
into the nature of practical theology as a theological discipline
and its place alongside the other theological disciplines. This
includes looking at the fundamental issue for the subject: the relation between theory and practice. The specific task of practical
theology is to reflect on Christian life and practice both within the
Church and within the wider society. Therefore practical theology
makes explicit that connection between theological understanding and faithful practice which is at the heart of all theological
activity.

In Part II attention is given to the processes involved in doing
practical theology. Thus there are chapters on methods of learn-

ing from experience, using different resources and the commitment to pastoral action. Practical theology facilitates the processes of theological engagement with concrete social and personal reality. This must include understanding and acquiring skills and insights. However, in the end practical theology, like all theology, is not simply about methodology or technology, but about growth in wisdom, spirituality, and the formation of men and women by the Spirit of Christ.

Such a book as this can only be an introduction. In order that the reader can relate to the relevant literature more readily, a basic initial bibliography has been provided. It is of course appreciated that this is only a starting point. The literature therefore is important and the student has to acquire the skills and information to explore the field. But practical theology is an academic as well as a practical subject which requires intellectual and critical exploration on the basis of good information and understanding.

At the same time practical theology is also rooted in the realities of actual human existence. For this reason the discussion arises from relevant case studies. While the persons and situations are not actual ones, nevertheless they represent real kinds of situation and experience. There are also fairly detailed suggestions and methods outlined for dealing with different aspects of doing practical theology. It is hoped, therefore, that it will provide a useful foundation for those who are being introduced to what is an exciting and expanding field of theological endeavour.

Paul Ballard and John Pritchard

Preface to the Second Edition

The reception of this book has been most encouraging. It has become one of the half-dozen standard texts in the field. There has been a wide readership and it has been recommended for courses in practical theology and/or ministerial training not only in the United Kingdom but in other parts of the English-speaking world.

However, in the decade since the first edition both the Church and society have seen many changes; though, by the same token, much remains very familiar. The original text, therefore, largely stands but has been revised in detail to relate it more closely to the present context. In two ways, however, there have been significant changes. A new chapter has been added reflecting the need to take account more directly of what we are now calling the post-modern world. The bibliographical information, too, has been updated and extended, without losing reference to the early literature which can be valuable for readers coming to the subject for the first time.

It is worth being reminded at this point what this volume is intended to do. It is primarily an attempt to address the pastoral and missiological task of relating to and thinking theologically in context. Practical theology is, by this token, defined not in the first instance in terms of skills or practices. These are, of course, necessary and need to be learned through the appropriate resources. Rather, it is defined as the theory and practice of theological thinking that should inform the spirituality and practice of the Christian community, its members and ministers, lay and ordained. If it succeeds in contributing to the enabling of this enterprise then this book will have fulfilled its task.

Paul Ballard and John Pritchard

Chapter 1

The significance of practical theology today

Christian theology has never been simply a speculative enquiry but a practical one. Theology is 'faith seeking understanding'. It arises from the experience of the life of discipleship and seeks to reflect on and serve that faith commitment. The root of all theology is the witness of the Christian community in worship, proclamation, service and daily living. So to be concerned with theology, not least practical theology, is to be part of the great stream of faith including those in the past who have struggled in their own day with what it meant to live as servants of Christ. It is their wisdom that we inherit as one of the resources for doing the same task in our own day.

However, practical theology is a particular field of theology. It specifically deals with Christian life and practice within the Church and in relation to wider society. Such a restrictive definition, however, is comparatively recent, stemming from the academic and cultural changes of the past three hundred years. This has also meant that practical theology has been somewhat marginalized from the main academic theological disciplines and often accorded a minor place in the theological pantheon. The days of being a Cinderella field in theology, however, seem to have ended. In recent decades there has been a revival in interest in practical theology. Indeed there are signs that it has moved onto centre stage. So to enter into the field of practical theology is to enter a growing and exciting area of study.

The expansion of practical theology

This resurgence of interest can be illustrated by the growth of activity on two fronts. First, there has been growth in the academic context. In 1970 some eight or nine teachers in the field met in Manchester at the instigation of Bob Lambourne and Jim Blackie. These two were pioneers from different sides of the border. Bob Lambourne had recently been appointed the first lecturer in Pastoral Studies at the University of Birmingham, a new departure in English and Welsh theology. Jim Blackie, Professor of Christian Ethics and Practical Theology in Edinburgh, was in the process of transforming that long established department by introducing new and varied courses alongside the traditional basic provision for training ordinands. Others have since followed. The whole process was significantly boosted by the rapid introduction of courses in pastoral theology and pastoral training in the theological colleges in the 1970s, especially among Anglicans.[1] The result is that the conference which has since met almost annually since 1970 has had fifty or more people present, drawn from a wide range of educational and other institutions and organizations. In 1994 the British and Irish Association for Practical Theology (BIAPT) was formally established. This continues to meet annually in July but has also been able to take some new initiatives such as initiating or sponsoring research. This followed the inauguration in Princeton, in 1993, of the International Academy for Practical Theology. The Academy's biennial meetings have been held in countries across the world, drawing together scholars from many cultures and traditions. Its proceedings have become resource material for appreciating the international dimensions of the subject. The International Society for Empirical Theology (ISET), with the *Journal of Empirical Theology*, based in Nijmegen, The Netherlands, provides a forum for those engaged in qualitative and quantitative research in areas of theological and pastoral concern. The field continues to expand.

Secondly, the developments in the academic world have been paralleled by other initiatives both within the churches and by concerned individuals or groups, of which two types are of interest here. The first has been in the field of pastoral care. A number of bodies emerged to promote standards and skills in pastoral work. We note, for example: the Scottish Pastoral Association, which founded the journal *Contact*, the leading journal in Britain in this field; the Clinical Theology Association, now the Bridge Pastoral Foundation, founded on the pioneering work of Frank Lake; the Westminster Pastoral Foundation, the brainchild of Bill Kyle and now at the heart of a national network of counselling centres; and the Association for Pastoral Care and Counselling which is part of the British Association for Counselling and Psychotherapy. More recently there has been a growing interest in chaplaincy in several spheres. Most notable has been the boom in health care chaplaincies. These, too, have their own associations.[2] Inter-disciplinary concerns were also sustained by such bodies as the Institute for Religion and Medicine and the Churches' Council for Healing. The second group of initiatives is less coherent, and can be brought together under the heading of 'Church and Society'. Here we can give examples such as: the Industrial Mission Association stemming from the pioneering work of Ted Wickham in Sheffield; Church Action on Poverty; the Churches' Community Work Alliance (CCWA); the Evangelical Coalition for Urban Mission (ECUM); the Urban Theology Unit, Sheffield (UTU); and the William Temple Foundation, Manchester (WTF). Such bodies, of which these are only examples, represent different aspects of Christian concern and action, bringing pressure to bear on the thought and practice of the churches, both severally and ecumenically.

The cultural context

All this growing activity arose from some fundamental changes in both the Church and wider society which have combined to thrust practical theology to the fore and to refashion or replace earlier practices.

First, there has been a **fundamental shift** in society. Christianity is no longer automatically assumed to be the normative expression of British culture. We now live in what is often referred to as a post-modern or post-Christian and increasingly pluralistic society in which different faiths, religious or humanistic, sit side by side in various states of co-operation or competition. One of the effects of this has been a growing feeling that the Christian community has to defend its own existence both institutionally and intellectually. Theology thus becomes an important resource in this search for Christian identity. It can no longer (if it ever did) function as a purely 'academic' or independent activity but must be seen to be contributing directly and practically to the life of Christian witness and service. In recent years, moreover, a strong interest in spirituality has emerged. This ranges from a revival of the Christian classical patterns to New Age or eastern religions. Once again the Christian community finds itself having to set out its stall anew in the open market. It is not surprising therefore that more and more theology is overtly described as 'practical', helping its students to understand their faith in the context of a changing world.

Secondly, especially during and since the Second World War, there has been a phenomenal rise of the **social sciences** and their related professions such as social work, therapy, counselling and education. This, of course, has meant that Christian faith has had to enter into dialogue with new intellectual challenges. But, as importantly, there have been obvious and direct practical implications. The Welfare State has demanded a difficult adjustment from the Church in relation to its social responsibilities, which is now, ironically, having to be re-negotiated. Government policy has increasingly shifted the emphasis from state benefit and support to private initiative and personal responsibility. This has meant the severe reduction and even collapse of some of the welfare structures. For example, in the case of Care in the Community, more and more of the burden is being transferred on to family support and commercial and voluntary organizations. As part of the new emphasis on voluntary groups and the desire to harness the co-operation of the so-called faith communities, the churches are being asked to pick up again many of the roles taken over by the Welfare State only a generation or so ago. This has, however, been coupled with increasingly stringent regulations covering all community and service provision, from disability to child protection.

Yet, at the same time, the caring professions have developed their own professional theory and skills. These now set the standards for good practice. They have therefore become models for the professional development of clergy and the enhancement of quality in Christian voluntary work. Practical theology has been at the forefront of taking up this task (though increasingly other branches of theology are being affected). This means that practical theology, in our time, could be said to be at the cutting edge of Christianity's encounter with important aspects of modern culture.

The third major change is linked to the other two but has a different character. It can be characterized as the **contextualization of theology**. Its best known exemplification is in the liberation theology of Latin America, but contextuality can be found in many shapes and guises.[3] The two marks of such a theological method are: the need to take the living context seriously as the root of and data for theological reflection; and the assumption that all theological activity is directed towards the practical end of witness and struggle for the Kingdom of justice and peace. Thus we find in Latin America and elsewhere theology rooted in 'base' communities in city slums or in areas of rural poverty. It is a theology that points to the power of the God who is found sharing the brokenness of the lives of people and communities. It is a theology which is more concerned with orthopraxis – that is, living out the struggle of faith – than with orthodoxy – that is, believing the right things. This suggests a major reorientation as to how theology functions: theology is essentially a practical enterprise. Theological reflection thus becomes part of action, something that is done in and with the whole Christian community. Such an approach has far-reaching effects. It has widely permeated, whether consciously or by osmosis, much practice in this country, not only in the grass roots of the Christian community but increasingly in the more formal theological activity of university and college.

At the same time two other theological approaches have emerged that underline the practical nature of the discipline. As part of the reaction to post-modernism and the subsequent search for Christian identity, stress has been laid on the distinctive and critical nature of Christian belief in a culturally plural society. This takes many forms and revives strands in Christian attitudes that have always been there. But it has perhaps been 'radical orthodoxy' that is its most stringent exemplar. From a different angle, not least from the biblical scholars, theology has been propounded as hermeneutics; that is, as a dialogue between text and context, tradition and contemporary practice. This has been taken up, not least in the form of 'story' by many in terms of pastoral practice.[4]

Such developments, however, leave us with a paradox, for two models for practical theology have emerged from the above discussion. Either it is a specialized branch within the wider field of theology, developing its own particular interests and tasks, with relevant skills and practices. Or it is the normative form of theology as such so that the practical is the formative focus of all theology. But these are not to be seen as necessarily mutually contradictory, although they can appear to pull in different directions. Perhaps it is necessary to live with the paradox. Indeed the assumption that is here being made and which will be sustained in the argument of the following chapters is that practical theology is indeed a discipline with its proper function within theology; but that this is not done in isolation from the other theological disciplines, for all theology is indeed essentially a single and practical activity. Practical theology therefore is the place where the reality of all theology as a practical discipline is clearly manifest. It is a primary witness to theology's essential task. It represents and shares in the common theological calling of all the other theological disciplines.

The expanding content of practical theology

The scope and purpose of practical theology has also been broadened in another way. It is no longer confined to preparation for ministry. Today people engage with practical theology for many reasons. They may have particular interests, such as a concern for the environment or conditions in the inner city. Or there may be a desire to meet the challenges and pressures of society and social trends. Or it may be that the aim is to grow in understanding of the life of discipleship in a given context – as teacher or manager or shopfloor worker. Or it may be that the insights and skills necessary for ministry, taken in a theological context, can be of use to those engaged in other forms of pastoral caring – such as youth work, counselling or nursing. Practical theology therefore is of interest to a wide range of people. It raises the theological issues of meaning and truth in relation to the living out of the life of faith. It brings together theory and practice. It relates to pastoral skills and ministerial training but is also concerned for every aspect of social policy and cultural experience.

In a field that is potentially so wide ranging it is necessary to find a means of limiting an introductory discussion. The focus here, therefore, will be on practical theology as a subject found in the more academic forms of theology. This is not to forget the wide range of activities and opportunities to do practical theology both inside and alongside the Church that also constitute an important part of the field. So, in Part I, we shall be looking at the place of practical theology in the spectrum of the whole range of theological subjects; and, in Part II, we shall take up the methods and strategies that we believe constitute the essential core of practical theology. The aim, therefore, is to provide an introduction to what practical theology is all about, thereby giving some coherence to what can appear to be a somewhat disparate discipline.

Notes

1 For an introduction to the subject in Britain see Ballard, Paul H., *The Foundations of Pastoral Studies and Practical Theology* (University College, Cardiff 1986); also relevant articles in *Contact*, such as those by Lambourne, R.A. (35, 1971) Gill, Robin (56, 1977) Lyall, David (65, 1979) Dyson, A.O. (56, 1977) Wharton, Martin (78, 1983) Pattison, Stephen (80, 1983) Elford, John (80, 1983) Wilson, Michael (87, 1985) Campbell, Alastair (88, 1985) Lartey, Emmanuel (112, 1993).

2 For introductions to some of the organizations mentioned, see relevant articles and reviews in *Contact*, such as 83, 85, 1984; 88, 1985; 89, 1986; 97, 1988; 100, 1989; 106, 1991. For chaplaincies see Legood, Giles, *Chaplaincy, the Church's Sector Ministries* (Cassell 1999); Swift, Christopher, *Contact* 144, 2004, for issues facing mental health chaplains.

3 The importance of liberation theology will be discussed later, in Chapter 5. For an introduction to the contextual mode of doing theology see Bevans, S.B., *Models of Contextual Theology* (Orbis 1992).

4 These are followed up in Chapter 5 but for radical orthodoxy see: Hyman, Gavin, *The Predicament of Post-modern Theology – Radical Orthodoxy or Nihilist Textuality?* (Westminster/John Knox 2001); and for hermeneutics in pastoral care see: Ballard, Paul and Holmes, Stephen R., *The Bible in Pastoral Practice* (Darton, Longman and Todd 2005); see also general bibliography.

PART I

The Foundations

Chapter 2

Practical theology as an academic discipline

Practical theology is problematic. The growing interest in the field has raised questions about its nature and purpose, its form and methodology. In what sense, it is asked, is practical theology a proper branch of theology at all, and if it is, where does it fit in?

For some, practical theology is not a real theological discipline. It is about practice. Its task is to teach people 'how' to operate in a given situation. The scholarly critical questions of 'why?' or 'whether?' tend to be missing. It is really only training, learning how to apply an already established belief. Practical theology therefore is not an open enquiry but a churchly activity, required for the professional training of ministers. Thus it is not a theological discipline on two counts:

(i)   it is application and not critical theory;
(ii) it is ecclesiastical and not academic.

But is this really so? The purpose of this chapter is to set practical theology within the spectrum of theological activity. First this means looking at the nature and purpose of theology itself. Practical theology is partly legitimized by being placed in a field of study which is essentially related to practice. Secondly, then, practical theology has to be given its own place within the range of theological disciplines: i.e. alongside biblical studies, systematics or Church history. Thirdly, we need in a preliminary way to describe how practical theology can be described as an academic, though practical, discipline. This is followed by looking at some of the ways practical theology manifests itself. Finally, a brief note tries to sort out some of the terminology involved.

The nature of theology

Tom had begun to settle down at university. It was his second week. Classes had sorted themselves out. He was going to enjoy doing his theology degree and found it easy to relate to his other classmates. One day, in the refectory at coffee break (which of course tended to stretch out),Tom asked some of his new friends why they were studying theology. Peter and Sue were quite clear. They were ordinands from a theological college, and for them it was part of their training. They were there to deepen their theological understanding in relation to the issues posed by the modern world. Angela sort of agreed; only her interest was teaching in schools. She guessed that later she would take up options in other religions. Nigel, however, saw it more as a personal quest. As a thoughtful Christian he wanted to put his faith on a more adequate foundation, to test it and work out its implications. Percy was the group clown, but he also had an academic purpose. He was not so sure about the truth of Christianity any more – but was glad to have a chance to examine his doubts and queries in a critical and open way. Besides, it was a good course, not presupposing any beliefs, allowing freedom of debate. Marjorie too had no religious background and no real faith. RE had been fun and interesting at school so she thought theology would be as good a liberal arts degree as any and at least she could ask all the serious questions while studying the roots of her own culture.

Listening to all this Tom began to realize that what they had been discussing was what Dr Smith had been saying only yesterday in a lecture. The group had been describing the nature and purpose of theology. To put it at its simplest, theology is thinking about faith. It tries to look at what faith means in a systematic way, to test its truth, to face the challenges posed to it by other faiths and other forms of knowledge, such as science or sociology, and to ask how Christian faith fits into and can express itself in the modern world. Theology therefore arises out of the community of faith. It serves the intellectual needs of that faith and is engaged in the dialogue concerning the truth and validity of the faith.

If this is so then we can characterize theology as a fourfold activity:

(i) Theology is a descriptive activity: on the basis of Scripture and tradition it describes how Christians have believed and still do believe in, and live out, their faith. In this sense it is phenomenological, similar to and part of the broader study of religion, not asking truth questions but the historical and socio-psychological questions of the human sciences.

(ii) Theology is a normative activity: that is, on the basis of Scripture and tradition, it seeks to establish the inner meaning of Christian belief, to examine its norms and claims, and then to examine both the thought and life of the Church in the light of its findings. Thus theology is a critical, prophetic activity calling the community of faith back to its essential commitment, challenging it in word and deed.

(iii) Theology is a critical activity. It lives on the frontiers of faith, responding to, sifting and working on the challenges posed by the insights of those engaged in other disciplines. It is concerned with questions of truth, its own and other people's truth.

(iv) Theology is an apologetic activity: that is, it is concerned to work out the implications, intellectual and practical, of the Christian faith.

All this can be summed up in Anselm's classic definition of theology: '*fides quaerens intellectum*' – faith searching for understanding.[1] Schubert Ogden describes theology as 'the fully reflective understanding of the Christian witness of faith as decisive for human existence'.[2]

Two implications, however, follow from such a description of theology. First, there is a necessary and fundamental tension here. On the one hand theology arises out of, and is there to serve, the Church, albeit in a critical and specialized way. This suggests that there is a kind of inner limitation to theology's freedom and independence. There is an issue of authority, since theology acts on behalf of and for the purposes of the People of God. In some traditions this is more clearly embedded in ecclesial structures than others. For instance, in Roman Catholicism, the teaching authority is found in the *magisterium*, that is, the Pope and the bishops. Theology's task is to provide support and encouragement. Theologians who appear to allow their critical activities to take them too far astray are restrained or, if thought to have gone beyond the bounds of the faith, have their licence to teach on behalf of the Church withdrawn.[3] In other traditions the process is less formalized but none the less real. Public church representatives are expected to sustain the normative tradition. When this appears to be undermined, voices of protest are heard, as David Jenkins discovered when he was Bishop of Durham;[4] or anxiety, such as that caused by the debate over homosexuality and ministry, is expressed. Yet, at the same time, theology is a genuinely academic subject in the sense that it is concerned with critical and open enquiry into truth, whether historical or metaphysical. It is engaged with scholarly activity and research within the market place of ideas of a university. Otherwise it could have no appeal to the sceptic or genuine enquirer and it would soon cease to explore new possibilities of faith and understanding in a changing world. Don Cupitt may be controversial, but as a theologian he has the right and the duty to push his thinking as far as he can within the public debate.[5] So, also, the debate about science and faith has to be brought out into the open. For theology to be true to itself it has to hold these two functions together: its roots in the community of faith and its freedom of enquiry. And if practical theology is to be a part of the theological spectrum, it too must be both at the service of the gospel in the Church and a resource for critical enquiry into Christian practice.

The second implication to be drawn from the nature of theology is that there is no sharp division between the academic and the practical. Theology, in its service of the community of faith, is essentially practical. All theological activity arises out of the words, deeds and institutional practice of the Christian story and is given back as a resource for further action in the service of the gospel. The relationship between theological study and its practical implications may not always be direct and clear. Yet, for instance, the scholarly and critical study of the New Testament is necessary if the Church is to live out the Scriptures with integrity; or the careful philosophical arguments concerning the truth and understanding of doctrine are what enable the preacher to speak with greater realism and relevance. Without the rigour of theological scholarship the everyday life of faith would soon show a lack of critical awareness and intellectual backbone. Again, the same has to be true of practical theology.

So practical theology must take on the characteristics of theology as such. It too is a descriptive, normative, critical and apologetic activity. It is the means whereby the day-to-day life of the Church, in all its dimensions, is scrutinized in the light of the gospel and related to the demands and challenges of the present day, in a dialogue that both shapes Christian practice and influences the world, however minimally.

Practical theology among the disciplines

Tom and his friends eventually have to stop sitting around and talking. Classes call. 'What's next?' enquires Angela. 'New Testament,' comes the reply. 'O bother!' exclaims Nigel. 'I've left that file at home.' 'Yes,' says Peter, 'my bookshelves have rows of files too. That's the only way I can keep the different subjects in a tidy order.'

Peter's remark represents what most students of theology find. Their course resembles a series of files, into which they place separate notes from different subjects. Each subject area seems to live in a more or less hermetic box. Study is broken up into what Edward Farley calls 'a plurality of specific disciplines'.[6] This gets worse at post-graduate level because then you tend to specialize in just one such discipline, becoming cut off from colleagues in other areas, and divided into what Farley calls 'scholarly guilds' each with its own professional organization and journals. Such a development is perhaps inevitable. Each theological discipline has expanded its own literature, and forged its own technical language. Just as nuclear physicists working in adjacent laboratories in different branches of the field find it hard to communicate professionally, so those in different theological disciplines can appear to live on different planets. The result can be that theology simply appears to be a random collection of topics only held together tenuously in a single degree programme. It is left to the student to make sense of the situation and to pull all the disparate parts together into a systematic whole: though whether it is often done is a matter of conjecture.

A great deal of attention, much of it creative and valuable, has been given to this issue. A lot of energy has been spent on trying to forge some coherent and structured courses. There does not seem, however, to be a tidy solution. On one hand, to create opportunities for cross-linking between subjects, or to have seminars and courses that allow exchange from one subject area to another, seems merely to add another layer to an already full programme. But on the other hand, to design a course round a guiding principle or aim, such as preparation for pastoral work or ordination, can so control the structure as to narrow it down unnecessarily or to constrict critical freedom. The classical expression of this latter approach was Schleiermacher's justification for academic theology as the professional training for clergy.[7] On his scheme, theology is given coherence by its aim. It starts with the foundations in theory and primary sources, leading to its application in ministry. But that narrows theology to what Farley calls 'the clerical paradigm', ignoring its other critical and thus distinctively academic functions.[8] Is there however another framework that can provide theology with coherence within a necessary openness? What is needed is a framework which can allow genuine freedom to the different disciplines yet provide them with a corporate rationale as collectively being theology. Moreover it must be a framework that is theologically grounded, so that it is justified in terms of its own existence and not determined by some kind of external criterion; something that can hold theology together in its descriptive, narrative, critical and apologetic tasks.

This is found in the fundamental claims made by Christianity. At the heart of the Christian faith is the person of Jesus Christ as the incarnate, crucified and risen Lord. This is held to be the clue to the nature of all reality, of God and creation. But belief in Christ as the primary revelation of God carries with it a number of significant implications. Christianity is an historical faith. Time and space are real. God has created us to know him within the limitations of our creatureliness.

Within the parameters of such a faith it is possible to begin to map out the inherent structure of theology. Perhaps the traditional disciplines are not so arbitrary after all. The primary disciplines are those that establish the faith: first of all in the historical reality of revelation – biblical studies; and secondly in the need to establish the grounds of faith in what may be called fundamental theology or philosophical theology. The wisdom of faith – developed through failure and success, in adversity and triumph, through sinful disobedience as well as by repentance and grace and heroic sanctity – is wrestled with in historical study. The demands of the present are taken up in systematic theology and practical theology which ask, respectively, 'What does it mean to believe Christianly today?' and 'What does it mean to live and act Christianly today?' But there is also an eschatological horizon.

The Kingdom has not yet come; so we ask how do we move into God's future and keep ourselves open to the possibility of newness and surprise. This allows for that critical openness that is essential for theology. But this is not to repeat Schleiermacher's scheme, moving from foundations to product. Rather it is to suggest that the whole theological enterprise acts like petals in a flower – each contributes to the whole and all are needed for a full bloom.

Each subject area, therefore, concentrates on its own contribution to the theological whole. Each is dependent on, draws on and services the work of the other. Thus for instance New Testament studies investigate the historical roots of the gospel. Yet this is not done in a vacuum but rather in the light of the history of interpretation, and conscious of its importance for dogmatics. Similarly, practical theology draws on the insights and challenges posed by historical and systematic theology in understanding practice and, at the same time, offers new perspectives on Bible and doctrine out of its experience. Practical theology, therefore, can be seen as having a proper and full part to play as a distinct discipline within the theological enterprise.

Practical theology as its own discipline

The place and shape of practical theology are beginning to emerge. The first section underlined the fourfold nature of theological activity as descriptive, normative, critical and apologetic. For practical theology, as for all other theological disciplines, the critical and exploratory nature of theology is crucial in its open, faithful service of the Church and the world. The second section suggested that this task was to be done alongside, and yet in solidarity with, all the other parallel kinds of theological activity. Here attention moves to ask what kind of discipline practical theology is. Any discipline will normally be seen to have three basic characteristics, though one or other will probably be more dominant in any given instance.

Subject area
First there needs to be a **recognized subject area**. This can be quite obvious, as in the case of New Testament studies. It is said that a professor of theology once persuaded a sceptical colleague to hear the inaugural lecture of the new professor of New

Testament studies. After the lecture the host turned to his friend to ask him what he thought of it. 'He has too little to do,' was the reply. Perhaps he was a bit harsh, but it makes our point: that subject, at least, has precise boundaries. But none are absolutely hard and fast, for they all impinge on other fields and are involved in other enquiries. So, for example, what are the bounds of church history? There is a fairly reasonable focus: the story of Christianity; but that is also part of and affected by the social, economic and political history of the culture within which the Christian faith is found.

Other disciplines are much more diffuse and better described as fields of study. This is true of practical theology. The subject matter is the practice of the Christian community within the world. This can embrace every dimension of Christian presence: the formal, institutional structures and the informal voluntary activity, the corporate and the personal, both that which goes on within the community of faith and also that which goes on as the Church impinges on and responds to the wider culture. Practical theology can incorporate ethics and mission, pastoral care and institutional activities, catechetics and worship. Thus practical theology is closer to geography or education. It is a field that has a clear justification as the enquiry into Christian practice. Indeed it could be called a field within the primary field of theology itself.

Methodology

Secondly, a subject must be shaped by **a recognized methodology**. A subject area that is tightly circumscribed, such as the New Testament, is likely to be more eclectic in its choice of method. Other disciplines are primarily described by their methodology. Chemistry analyses all matter in accordance with its own procedures; mathematics is essentially a logical process that can be used in a wide variety of contexts. Within theology the philosophy of religion is understood as testing the meaning and truth of faith using recognized critical tools.

Practical theology, first of all, shares, with the rest of theology, the descriptive, normative, critical and apologetic tasks. Thus it draws on the basic theological method. It asks of the concrete practice of the Christian community: how does this situation, practice or action in the world express the gospel? Does it do so adequately or should it be challenged? Are we learning from this context? What should be said or done or urged in the name of the gospel in and for the world? In other words, practical theology raises the question of the presence of the Kingdom of God in our history. This is done alongside the other theological disciplines that inform it and are informed by it.

This will become clearer as we expound the methodology of practical theology in Part II around the concept of the pastoral cycle. Here a brief illustration will have to suffice. Reinhold Niebuhr found his ministry changed when, as a young pastor in Detroit, he was himself caught up in controversy through having to respond to a strike at Fords. He learnt of the hardships of working class life – the long hours, low wages, bad housing, harsh management practices, and the consequent hopelessness and degradation. As he encountered the pastoral and social realities he found that he was compelled in the name of justice to get actively involved in the socio-economic realities, and to challenge the system that created them. Only thus could the gospel be heard. But that had a personal knock-on effect, for his preaching and pastoral work had to change to accommodate his newly found dimension of the social gospel.[9] This was to lead him to be one of the most influential theologians of the 1930s and 1940s.

Secondly, however, because of its focal concern for Christian practice, practical theology draws on the methodologies of the social sciences as its critical partners. Here are its basic tools for understanding the social reality in which we are set and which has to be served in the name of Christ. All theological disciplines employ critical tools from other disciplines. In biblical studies for example, it is the tools of historical analysis and criticism, and literary critical methods; or in systematic theology it is philosophy.

Critical and practical

Thirdly, all subjects are **both critical and practical**. On the one hand there is the search for truth, the delight in discovery and pushing back the frontiers of knowledge and enquiry. This is the Everest syndrome. One climbs it because it is there and the struggle is to overcome the obstacles set by the mountain itself. Mathematicians tell us that there is a pure aesthetic joy in their work that does not depend on application.[10] All academic work carries with it a sense of its own intrinsic worth. The search for understanding may start with faith and intend to serve faith but it has also to be given freedom of pursuit and expression. This freedom is the foundation of critical openness.

Usually, however, there is also an element of purpose, even in the most dispassionate enquiry. So a scientist probably embarks on a series of experiments because somewhere there is a link into a possible application. The sociologist, for example, takes up an issue because it is already of some importance in society. Some disciplines, like education, social work or practical theology, have the practical in the forefront.

Faith, practice and society
There can however be a tension between the demands of critical openness and the desire to be useful. This can be illustrated by the debate concerning religious sociology. The sociology of religion is the sociological study of religion in society, irrespective of the nature or truth of religion and unconnected with pastoral aims or practice. It aims to provide a disinterested description of the religious situation studied. On the other hand, religious sociology (a term taken from the French *sociologie réligieuse* where it has had a long tradition in Catholic circles) is the use of sociological methods to identify possible options for pastoral or ecclesial practice. It is closer to market research. Church growth studies would be a current example, in which sociological theory is used to serve a theologically determined aim. Some sociologists see a sharp and absolute distinction between these. Others, however, point out that no sociological research is done purely altruistically. Indeed much social enquiry is actively commissioned. But it is equally true that so-called research which does not have a critical depth to it can sometimes miss crucial factors and information because the practical interest had narrowed the focus too far. Both are necessary, so that inevitable partiality is countered by critical openness.[11]

The nature of practical theology as a discipline which this section has tried to describe has been well summed up by James Whyte:

> The systematic theologian asks critical questions about the way faith expresses itself in language; the practical theologian asks critical questions about the way faith expresses itself in practice and about the relation between the practice and the language. Since the Church's life and action is related not only to its self-understanding and comprehension of its faith, but also to the changing society in which it functions, practical theology is

triadic, concerned with the inter-relationship of faith, practice and social reality and is aware that the lines of force flow in both directions.[12]

Variations on a theme

Practical theology serves the life and work of the Christian community in its witness and service in and for the world. In common with all theology, it is a descriptive, normative, critical and apologetic activity, with its subject matter being the life and practice of the Church and the outworking of the gospel in every aspect of human community. Its field therefore is almost limitless. There is no human activity that is not properly open to theological scrutiny. Its task is to reflect on the presence in the world of God as creator, redeemer and sustainer. But such an agenda cannot be undertaken comprehensively. It can surely only be taken up piecemeal, according to the demands, expectations and resources of a particular situation. Does this not mean once again that we are faced, as in theology as a whole, with the tension between the various specialized interests and the need to have cohesion, and with the accusation that practical theology is really only a rag-bag of loosely related disciplines?

This was the question that was going round Gerry's mind as he sat in his discussion group. He was attending a conference for practical theologians. As he looked round there were familiar faces as well as new faces. In the introductions they had said what they were doing. Anne and Jason, like Gerry, taught in theological colleges, training clergy. Anne was a social worker now teaching pastoral care, while Gerry and Jason had worked in a parish or congregation in the inner city. Julian, however, worked in a university department teaching ethics both to the theological students and, interestingly, to nurses and social workers. Hannah was a parish worker and a counsellor and ran the voluntary local counselling service. Luke was a parish priest but concerned, in his industrial context, about poverty and practical Christian witness. Janice, too, was engaged in industrial mission and was seeking opportunity for theological reflection; while Jim was a hospital chaplain engaged in asking questions about health and human society. Gerry could see how in some way each was engaged in practical theology but it was difficult to see how the group could really find much common ground. Some were more concerned with skills and pastoral insights, some with society and its life, others with theological reflection and others with spirituality. Yet they were all there because they each understood themselves to be engaged in practical theology.

Practical theology, therefore, manifests itself in a myriad ways, of which Gerry's group was a kind of microcosm. It ranges from university departments and theological colleges and courses to structures of pastoral and community concern; from the task of teaching and academic discussion to the everyday task of ministry in parish or specialized fields. It is possible however to suggest that there are three main models for practical theology relating to the following: professional formation, the life of the whole people of God and the wider life of society.

Professional formation

If you ask what practical theology is about, the most usual answer from church members would be 'the training of ministers, priests and clergy'. This is, after all, the traditional expression of the subject as it emerged within the 'theological encyclopaedia'.[13] It is also the most clearly defined area, with institutional boundaries, recognized activities and a concerted purpose.

Yet even here all is not plain sailing. When Susan entered theological college she was surprised to find that her timetable contained a number of discrete topics: worship and liturgy, preaching and education, pastoral care and counselling, church management and leadership, church and society, community work, evangelism and mission. These ran side by side, each apparently understood as an essential dimension of ministry. Apart from the usual divorce between biblical and doctrinal studies and practical courses, practical theology itself was divided up.

This is further complicated by a division between two different kinds of discipline within practical theology. There are those, like pastoral care, that have tended to be dependent on the human sciences and their related professional models and skills. This has raised the problems of how to move from a dependence on such resources to a dialogue with other more explicitly theological disciplines. In recent years, however, there has been a decisive attempt to recover an openness to Scripture and tradition in doing practical theology, in both mainstream and liberal circles as well as among more conservative elements, both evangelical and catholic.[14] The other approach found within practical theology has been to start with the theological tradition and move towards the practical. This is the tendency when looking at issues concerning formal, traditional church practices. The result has been, sometimes, an excessive dependence on historical precedent and a theological prescriptiveness which can be insensitive to the importance of the social and psychological realities. A good example is found in the important World Council of Churches' document *Baptism, Eucharist and Ministry*. This statement could prove to be one of the classic texts of the Church in the search for doctrinal unity. Yet, for all its qualities, it has an abstract, timeless feel about it which, on occasion, misses the historical human reality.[15] There does not appear to be much recognition of the importance of the social context for the shaping of theological understanding.

The other problem which bothered Susan emerged in a conversation with Andy. For Andy the importance of these classes was what he called 'tools for the job'. His concern was to be given skills and techniques so that he could get stuck into ministry. He had an 'instrumental' view of all this training. Susan, on the other hand, while not despising the real value of training in skills and methods, saw the value of the course in allowing her to explore the groundwork of ministry, to lay a foundation of conceptual and critical understanding on which she could draw as need arose. That would provide a broad basis from which to be able to see her particular situation in context and to know which skills or insights to acquire when on the job. So she saw real value in the introduction to social theories or in the periods of exploration into theological and other questions. They made her think so that, even now, in her church placement she recognized that she was aware of the complexities and possibilities of any given pastoral situation.

What Stephen Pattison calls 'the seduction of relevance'[16] is a perennial problem. So too is the 'flight into abstraction'. Andy wanted all the time to know how any piece of work was 'relevant', by which he meant obviously and immediately useful. What Susan was looking for was the opportunity to weave a pattern of connections between all the different fields of learning and practice she was encountering, without diminishing the value and importance of each. And to do this in such a way that she herself would grow both as a person and as the minister she was training to be. This is, indeed, the most difficult of all tasks. There is no sure way to guarantee that it happens. But it is the primary task of all practical theology as a process of professional formation; one that has constantly to be assessed and reaffirmed.

The whole people of God

One of the most significant recent developments in the life of the churches has been the rediscovery of the laity as the people of God. This is most vividly demonstrated within Roman Catholicism as one of the fruits of the Second Vatican Council (1965–8).[17] The emphasis is on the idea of the pilgrim people, sharing in a common life of witness and service, focused on the eucharistic fellowship. This transforms the notion of ministry. There are many different ministries, formal and informal, alongside the sacramental ministry. Indeed all the baptized are committed in their personal, family, work and community life to the fundamental ministry of witness to the presence of Christ in the world.[18] This was one of the early concerns of the World Council of Churches, embodied in the so-called laity movement, and more recently the charismatic movement, with its stress on the diversity of gifts within the body of Christ, has also rediscovered the same theme.[19]

This emphasis has had a number of effects. First there is a widespread interest in theological learning. Theology and religious studies attract more and more students, and evening classes and other part-time educational facilities appear to prosper. Secondly, however, there is a corresponding increase in interest in practical theology. At the more formal end, more and more theological colleges include students who are not intending ordination but are seeking other spheres of service or who wish to acquire theological training for its own sake. This is also true of the part-time courses, originally founded for the equipping of ordinands but which have now broadened their intake.[20] A third pattern that has emerged in a number of forms is what might be called 'theological reflection' courses. A clear example is the growing availability of Masters' courses that offer the chance to study theological themes and issues in the context of ministry or other experience. The same kind of opportunity is also offered in shorter courses or in less structured group settings.[21]

Such developments have broadened the concepts of theological education considerably. There is, however, a serious danger. By becoming more diffuse, and in a context in which DIY religion has become all too common and traditional authorities have been weakened, there is a tendency for much so-called theology to work with somewhat under-informed, romantic and experimentalist models that can make somewhat naive, even dangerous, connections. Post-modernist pluralism and New Age mysticism might suggest that we each weave our own spirituality according to our own pattern. This suggests, therefore, that care and judgement are needed.

The wider society

Practical theology, in its modern expression, has also expanded in another direction. Christianity makes universal truth claims about the nature of the world and of human life. Therefore there has always been a concern for every aspect of our existence – from personal behaviour to politics and economics, from the creative arts to the sciences and technology. This has traditionally been expressed in the theological spectrum in the study of Christian ethics. In the context of the present discussion, however, two points need to be made concerning this field in relation to practical theology. The first is to note the way traditional areas of study have often been broadened and brought into alliance with other, often professional, interests. So, for example, it is possible to share common ground with other caring professions and to offer common courses on professional ethics. The ordinand may be in the same class as nurses, doctors or social workers. Or the lecturer may be delivering courses to several different but parallel groups. Or again, there can be ways of linking concerns about ecology, technology or the nature of scientific enquiry that are found among theologians, philosophers, scientists and economists.

The second has been the way nationally and locally that social concerns have become very much part of the Church agenda. This has been taken up through such bodies as Boards of Social Responsibility, or in national reports such as *Faith in the City*.[22] There are also various organizations concerned for ministry in various areas, such as industry, poverty or race relations, that stimulate theological debate and challenge the Christian community to take its responsibilities seriously. Thus, albeit often in symbolic ways, the Church is found to be engaged with human life in all its aspects. Practical theology stands at the frontier between faith understanding the world and faith in action.

What's in a name?

It must already be apparent that practical theology can go under many guises and be called by many names. Nor is it always clear whether the different terms are to be used synonymously or as indicating subtle but real differences. So, the student may find a course called practical theology, or pastoral theology or ministerial studies. Does this matter? Ought some effort be made to regularize the usage? The present situation, reflecting the kaleidoscopic changes of the past, is a product of history rather than logic.

In Scotland, typically of the Reformed tradition, there have long been departments of practical theology, though sadly, with recent cuts in educational finances these have sometimes been amalgamated into joint units with doctrine and/or history. But the discipline, though traditionally linked with ministerial training, is now normally understood in the broader sense indicated above. Training for ministry is a sub-set within the field, often with its own qualifications, such as a Diploma in Ministry, where the subject area is not part of a more general theological degree. In England and Wales practical theology was almost unknown and only came into the university in the 1960s as pastoral studies. This title was a deliberate attempt to show its link with the caring professions and to suggest its inter-disciplinary nature by not putting theology into a privileged position. However, when the denominations, notably the Church of England, introduced greater professional demands in ministerial training, not least in the field of pastoral care, this too was called pastoral studies. The desire in this instance was to differentiate it from pastoralia (or hints and tips) and pastoral theology (the perception of ministry). But pastoral studies can also refer to the whole ministerial activity and thus be more inclusive. Meanwhile the term 'pastoral' has come to be used in secular personal care as (e.g.) developed in schools and universities. In English and Welsh theological education there are now signs of the introduction of the term 'practical theology'. This would not only bring it in line with the Scottish usage, but with a broader tradition, and relate it to the current debate in North America concerning the form, content and method of the discipline.

There is, thus, no clear-cut usage. The same term can be used for different things; and similar things be called by different names. Nevertheless, it is possible to discern something of a pattern which, while it may not become normative, is a useful working guide.

(a) **Practical theology** designates the whole field and is a primary theological discipline alongside biblical studies, Church history, systematics and fundamental theology.

(b) **Pastoral studies** usefully indicates (i) an interdisciplinary reflective activity, especially in certain university courses, usually of theology and pastoral practice in relation to the social sciences; and (ii) the study that supports pastoral care in ordained ministry; and (iii) more rarely, the study that supports the whole range of ministerial activity.

(c) **Pastoral theology** is (i) ministerial studies; or (ii) the theological underpinning of pastoral ministry embracing the concern of the whole people of God and thus part of the wider horizons of pastoral studies or professional ministerial studies.

(d) **Ministerial studies** is self-explanatory, and usually part of practical theology.

(e) **Pastoralia**, now outmoded, is a basic introduction to the nuts and bolts of ministerial practice.

(f) The word **pastoral**, therefore, tends to be used when the focus is on (i) ordained ministry; or (ii) personal care, sometimes in a secular form.[23]

Notes

1   Anselm (Archbishop of Canterbury 1093–1109). See Barth, K., *Anselm-Fides Quaerens Intellectum* (tr. Robertson, I.W., SCM 1960).

2   Ogden, Schubert, *On Theology* (Harper & Row 1986), p. i.

3   In recent years there have been several incidents but the classic cases have been those of Hans Küng and Leonardo Boff.

4   See Jenkins, David and Rebecca, *Free to Believe* (BBC Books 1991).

5   For an introduction to Cupitt's thought see Cowdwell, Scott, *Atheist Priest?* (SCM 1988). On science and religion see McGrath, A.E., *Science and Religion – an Introduction* (Blackwell 1999); Polkinghorne, J., *Belief in God in an Age of Science* (Yale 1998); and *Science and Theology* (Fortress 1998).

6   Farley, Edward, *Theologia* (Fortress 1983), p. 4.

7   Schleiermacher, F., *A Brief Outline on the Study of Theology*, tr. Tice, T. (John Knox 1966).

8   Farley, op. cit., p. 85.

9   See Darkin, Kenneth, *Reinhold Niebuhr* (Chapman 1989).

10 See Coulson, C.A., *Science and Christian Belief* (Fontana 1961).
11 Ballard, Paul H., *The Foundations of Pastoral Studies and Practical Theology* (University College, Cardiff 1986), p. 92. See Gill, Robin, *The Social Context of Theology* (Mowbray 1975), p. 24. Ven, Johannes van der, *Practical Theology* (Kok Pharos 1992) is a good contemporary example of religious sociology.
12 Whyte, James, in Campbell, Alastair, *A Dictionary of Pastoral Care* (SPCK 1987), p. 213.
13 See Farley, op. cit., pp. 56–66.
14 See Campbell, Alastair, *Rediscovering Pastoral Care* (Darton, Longman and Todd 1981); Pattison, Stephen, *A Critique of Pastoral Care* (SCM 2000). This provides a good survey of the field with bibliographical notes. Ballard, Paul and Holmes, Stephen R. *The Bible in Pastoral Practice* (Darton, Longman and Todd 2005).
15 *Baptism, Eucharist and Ministry* (WCC 1982).
16 Pattison, op. cit., p. 80.
17 *Vatican Council II – The Conciliar and Post-conciliar Documents* (Fowler Wright 1981), ed. Flannery, Austin: *Lumen Gentium*.
18. See Davey,Theodore, in Ballard, op. cit., pp. 19–25.
19 See Bliss, Kathleen, *We the People* (SCM 1963), for the laity movement of the 1950s and *We believe in the Holy Spirit* (Church House Publishing 1991), for the charismatic movement. More recent discussions include: Etchells, Ruth, *Set My People Free* (Fount 1995); Lakeland, Paul, *The Liberation of the Laity* (Continuum 2003).
20 See Vaughan, Patrick H., *Training for Diversity of Ministry* (University of Nottingham 1983).
21 Such courses, both at first degree and masters level, have proliferated (almost alarmingly) since the deregulation of the universities in 1993. One impetus has been the resurgence of conservative theology provided by institutions that are 'tradition specific'. See: Ballard, Paul, *Practical Theology, Proliferation and Performance* (RELIG, Cardiff University, 2001).
22 *Faith in the City* (Church House Publications 1985). *Faith in the Countryside* (Churchman 1990).
23 See Ballard, *Foundations*, pp. 146–50.

Chapter 3

The practical theologian

The nature and form of practical theology as a theological discipline has begun to emerge. It focuses on the life of the whole people of God in the variety of its witness and service, as it lives in, with and for the world. It asks questions concerning Christian understanding, insight and obedience in the concrete reality of our existence. It is, therefore, a theological activity, descriptive, normative, critical and apologetic, serving both the Church and the world in its reflective tasks. But practical theology is both a range of specific activities, relating to different aspects of the Church's life in the world, and a primary mode of theological activity, rooting all theology in its existential responsibility. It both has its own tasks and is representative of the whole. It is often illuminating, however, alongside such a fairly abstract, schematic description to ask also how it works out in practice. How people see themselves actually functioning tells us as much and more about the task as any job description. So this chapter aims to explore further the nature of practical theology by coming at it from the experience of the practitioner. But who is the practical theologian? What is the shape of the task? What is the hidden agenda that is so often the core reality?

Charles has been Director of Pastoral Studies at St Ulric's for three years. He has just accepted an invitation to speak at his local Anglican Diocesan Clergy School. The theme is 'Updating on Theology' and he has been asked to do the practical theology slot. This he feels is the perfect opportunity for reflecting on what has happened to him in the past three years. What has he learned? What does he now want to say about his task? Charles recognizes that he has indeed changed a lot since coming to St Ulric's;

though he can also see that much of what he now takes for granted had roots back in his experience as a parish priest and indeed elsewhere. Some of his more recent thinking is a kind of reversion to earlier foundations, rediscovered and reworked.

Perhaps, therefore, the way to approach this present assignment is to be somewhat biographical; all the more because the core of what he wants to say is that the practical theologian, while having specific tasks and expertise within the ordering of the life of the Christian community, is more truly understood as a focal person, someone who is there to enable the process of theological reflection which is at the heart of practical theology. To get that across and to widen his colleagues' understanding of who is involved would be really useful – especially since many of those who will be at the conference will be involved in placements and field work with his students. So Charles settles down with his note pad and begins to jot down his personal pilgrimage and to shape up his talk.

The practical theologian among colleagues

Charles remembered a remark from one of the churchwardens from his last parish at the farewell dinner given for him and his family. 'Well,' he said, 'you will be moving on to higher things.' To move into the world of university and college, it is widely assumed by the laity, is to come to grips with real theology and to be dealing more directly with the heart of the matter. To some extent Charles had shared that expectation and had gone along with the idea that it was a form of promotion. And it had been exciting and stimulating to work alongside others who were experts in their field and to get involved in discussion and to have one's mind stretched.

But now he would want to be quite emphatic: it is not a greater or lesser sphere of activity but a different one with its own demands and criteria. Theological structures may be very specialized but they are only one part (though necessary and important) of the complex life of the people of God. Yet the particular tasks of the theological structures (themselves very varied in form and competence) have their own shape and purpose. Charles in fact found himself in two such structures: the university and the college. In the university he was comparatively marginal as his subject was not offered to any extent, though he did some teaching in the psychology of religion. In the college he had a clear training role. Both structures were in fact important, despite some tension between them.

The university represented very forcibly the need for academic freedom, the ability to pursue knowledge for its own sake, unfettered by practical expectations or prejudged orthodoxy. As a practical theologian Charles had once again, as in his own now distant student days, been brought to see the importance of being challenged by new perspectives and insights. He had always accepted the need for high standards and honesty. In his own specialized skills in pastoral counselling he had recognized the need for a broad and thought out theoretical base. He was grateful, therefore, for opportunities to attend seminars and to listen to visiting lecturers.

Michael Taylor makes a very similar point:

All I wish to do now is to record my own experience of my own university faculty as a partner in the theological enterprise which for me reaches its proper fulfilment in the theological work of the people of God. I appreciate, not uncritically I hope, three aspects of that partnership. First, the university constantly reminds me of the need for a certain intellectual rigour . . . Secondly, the university may pursue certain enquiries for its own sake or for nobody's sake, certainly not always for the sake of the people, but from which I nevertheless benefit and on which I am to some extent parasitic . . . Third, the university . . . fulfils its responsibility by being somewhat irresponsible and producing material which is not what the church could have judged to be most relevant, so jolting its perspectives from an independent point of view.[1]

But this critical freedom is a necessary part of theology and therefore an essential dimension of the practical theologian's perspective. It is hard for the practical theologian not to be sucked into the immediate expectations and pressures of any situation rather than to have a truly critical engagement. Irresponsible critical detachment – the ivory tower syndrome – can be worse than useless, but so too can unthinking uncritical activism. Theological discernment demands both commitment and perspective.

The other half of the equation for Charles is represented by St Ulric's. Charles' appointment was by the college council but he had to have the approval of the bishop to undertake a recognized form of ministry. The college was founded for the training of ministers (though nowadays this can include other ministries apart from traditional ordination). The students come committed and expectant, seeking a curriculum designed to equip them for their life ahead. And those institutions that use the college, notably the churches, lay down certain requirements and validate the courses. As a practical theologian Charles is more closely identified with these expectations than some of his colleagues. He is held responsible for ensuring that students are given a relevant grounding in areas that will serve their practice. Of all theological disciplines practical theology is demand-led.

Nor is this inappropriate, if properly understood; for theology, especially practical theology, is there for the service of the Church in its life of witness and service. It is part of the dialectic of theology both to respond to, and to address, the community of faith. It is appropriate, therefore, for the practical theologian to be engaged in relevant practice, at national, regional and local level, working with others in the service of the Kingdom in the world. For Charles this meant being part of a local congregation, with occasional duties; but also he was a member of the local ecumenical planning group, a consultant for a counselling service and on a national working party which, from time to time, took him to London and elsewhere. It is not so easy, however, to sustain both poles of this dialectic: the freedom along with the acceptance of authority, the ability to question and challenge along with loyalty to the gospel in the Church. But this is the tension within theology which is to be found representatively in the person of the practical theologian who is both committed and open, faithful and critical.

The normal structures of theological education make another demand. It is not long into a conversation before Charles is inevitably asked: 'What do you teach?' For one of the expectations is that theologians work in different fields and have specific expertise. At one level Charles has no problem with this. Presumably he had been appointed because, besides his ministerial experience, he had trained in counselling and had developed a counselling centre in his last parish. Pastoral care and the introduction to counselling skills, supported by some understanding of the processes of human socialization and interpersonal relationships, have long been deemed a fundamental requirement of ministry. He was, therefore, the designated expert in that field, working alongside Margaret, who taught Church and society and community work, together with others dealing in topics ranging from liturgy to management, from evangelism to education. Within the local grouping of theological training centres, too, Charles provided the courses in pastoral care.

At another level, however, there is a major issue involved here. It is a constant complaint that the theological syllabus can be totally fragmented into a series of specialisms. For practical theology this can be a double problem. Not only are experts meant to concentrate on their expertise, but practical theology can seem to be at some distance from the centre of theological concerns. But this is to contradict the essential nature of practical theology as a theological activity. Its primary task is precisely to focus the whole theological enterprise on the demands, hopes, fears and actual practices of the community of faith so that its life in the world may be faithful to the gospel and relevant to its time. It is the task of the practical theologian not only to know the Church and the world as it is, but also to stand at that point where the concerns of the Church and the world meet in creative encounter exploring the perceptions of the gospel. That is, the primary task of the practical theologian is to facilitate theological reflection. This means enabling the interests, insights and challenges of the different elements of the theological enterprise to inform, and be informed by, the concrete reality of the present.

Thus, in answer to the question, 'What do you teach?', the practical theologian does not have a particular skill. The practical theologian only has a task (which is as open as it possibly can be) to include both theology and the present reality. Perhaps in a world that demands clear answers, this task is to be invisible and insecure, dependent entirely on the willingness of others to join in and participate. The task may even appear to be without substance or support so that it can be dismissed as non-existent. It is worse than being a 'jack-of-all-trades', for the practical theologian is trying to get others to cross boundaries and to listen to strange voices. He has to become an enabler, a go-between, trying to create a culture of theological thinking and acting.[2]

Charles has found developing a good programme of theological reflection one of the hardest parts of the job. Gradually, through trial and error and by recognizing that each situation had to be taken seriously, he has begun to build a tradition and an expectation. No longer are glib banalities enough. Theological reflection demands a rigour comparable to any other theological study. Moreover, he has begun to find allies who are glad to give time and effort to the task. Judith came especially to mind. It was after sharing a seminar that she expressed her delight in doing so because her own expertise in feminist and liberation theology could so easily become a descriptive, abstract exercise in a university setting. But here, in a practical theology seminar, it was possible to engage theologically with the living experience of people in a more direct way.

Or there was Bill, who taught church history and liturgy and who had lately become keen on the attempts to draw worship, pastoral care and congregational development together. As is so often the case, Bill had usually approached the problems of worship from the end of doctrine and tradition. He rightly claimed that worship should enshrine the faith and not be a matter of whim or instant reaction. The needs of the present find their place in the framework of the given liturgical structure. Pastoral care, on the other hand, tended to start from the other end, from the immediate situation. But as time went on it became clearer to Bill that both needed each other and there was a fruitful enlargement in comprehension and practice as worship and pastoral concerns informed each other.

There was, however, another group of people that Charles worked with closely: those who regularly or occasionally contributed to the work of practical theology from other disciplines or professions, especially the caring professions. It was always surprising and gratifying how readily so many different people gave of their time and expertise. There were here, however, two areas of anxiety.

The first was represented by a disconcerting conversation with a lecturer in social work. For her the clergy as ministers are some kind of amateur allies for the social worker. So what her department had to give, she was suggesting, was a whole range of professional skills to equip the ordinands, men and women, for their task. The religious element was purely fortuitous. Nor was such an incident isolated. Charles remembered the splendid GP in his first parish who took him under his wing as a young priest and inducted him into family therapy. Charles had also found a constant string of requests either for some special skills to be incorporated in the training or for a special need to be addressed in the already over-stretched pastoral programme. Only this term, there were approaches from youth work, bereavement counselling, the environmentalists, debt management, AIDS and child abuse care agencies plus more demands to respond to the requirements of fresh government legislation. Charles was somewhat amused when, at a meeting to consider one of these requests, he had heard a colleague mutter, 'Join the queue!'

This fervour to recruit the clergy and the theological student is in part the desire among hard-pressed agencies and crusading groups to recruit allies in the voluntary sector. The churches and their ministers are, by definition, heavily engaged in community service. In part also, this comes from the pressure towards professionalization whereby bodies in the caring business demand qualifications and training. This challenges the apparent amateurism of the ministry. The agencies want to help improve the competence of ministers. But this can create a sense of guilt at being marginalized. So there is a pressure to enter into what appears to be the security of recognized structures and professional skills. For some clergy this has meant moving out of ministry into one or other of these areas of service, or to turn ministry itself into a specialized service, such as pastoral counselling or community work.

Charles had no intention of belittling the value that has been found in learning from other fields in the caring professions. But perhaps it is the essential role of the clergy not to be identified with this or that role. Rather, it is important to be, like Hije Faber's clown or court jester, free and almost irresponsible, crossing the given boundaries, asking the challenging questions, building contacts where none have existed.[3] It is one of the contributions of industrial mission to insist that the chaplain goes into the factory as a guest, invited by both sides, union and management. It is important not to be identified with anyone but to win one's way by virtue of becoming accepted, defining the role in terms of a fundamental loyalty to the Kingdom.[4]

It is not easy to be the amateur. At their best, amateurs are highly skilled and well informed, working at the highest levels of competence. But they owe nothing to anyone and are free to work across the grain of the established forms. It could be that part of the function of the practical theologian is precisely to help resist the temptations of professionalization and to insist on the centrality of the less tangible but higher priority. The gospel seeks to

engage the whole person in the service of the Kingdom of God in
the setting of the whole of contemporary society. Excessive professionalization can narrow down the field of responsibility and
only engage a segment of personal reality. These limitations too
have to be worked at and overcome.

There is yet a deeper point. The insights, skills and purposes
that are being made available from the other caring professions
also carry with them a baggage of often undeclared assumptions
about human nature and human values. For example, Peter
Bellamy is very cautious about the pastoral use of much current
counselling theory and practice:

> Aspects of existential humanism undergird this system [i.e. of
> humanistic psychology] and create theological problems. As a
> basis for counselling in a Christian context much humanistic
> psychology is unacceptable. It is hostile to fundamental Chris-
> tian beliefs and practices.[5]

It is all too easy to take on board a whole scheme of theory and
practice without any real theological critique. There are tensions
here that cannot be avoided. It is a matter of much current debate
in practical theology. The practical theologian is thus caught up in
a process of dialogue: discovering more about the world and the
gospel in the light of new knowledge and better practice; while
also bringing to bear on all situations the wisdom of the tradition
and the insights of faith. This is a two-way process, albeit that the
Christian community always seems to be on the defensive. It is
the prerogative of the clown to think the unthinkable and to say it.
Charles remembered with pleasure two remarks. One came from
his own student days when a prominent economist claimed, 'I
always read the Christians, for they see things whole.' The other
was by a lecturer from another department who said she always
enjoyed teaching the theologians. 'They always keep you on your
toes. They ask unusual but fundamental questions that make one
go back to first principles.' Here, Charles reckoned, were the
hidden rewards of being a theologian. Perhaps here too was a
message of encouragement for his colleagues in ministry in the
field who felt marginalized and depressed.

Students and pastors

From considerations such as these it is possible to begin to sketch in an outline of the practical theologian. On the one hand there is a recognizable structure. A particular job will be shaped according to the expectations and demands of the situation. For Charles it was to provide with a team of colleagues the necessary training for ministry, within which his own specialization was pastoral care. This included arranging various learning experiences, from lectures and seminars to practicals, which together constituted a programme of training within a broader theological curriculum.

On the other hand, there is a more diffuse, less tangible dimension that is hard to define but which in fact constitutes the heart of the practical theologian's task. It is this that is the explicitly theological task – to participate in the theological reflection which brings together the living reality of the gospel with the issues, experiences and present existence of the Church and the world. The practical theologian, therefore, while working alongside other theological disciplines, is the focus for and witness to a primary theological function that draws together and gives direction to the whole theological enterprise – namely equipping the household of God to understand itself better as the witness to the God found in Christ in the service of his creatures. The practical theologian strives to be a bridge across a divide; a catalyst stimulating change and renewal; an enabler, who allows others to take up responsibilities; an educator who opens up the world to students within the community of shared learning.[6] Of course there are set occasions and structured means to facilitate this process of theological reflection but it is essentially an ongoing process of shared living. It is always a vulnerable and exposed position appearing to have no status or substance other than the wisdom and skills that are learnt in the doing. The practical theologian is essentially on pilgrimage with and for the people of God.

Charles knew that he had, in a peculiar sense, travelled a full circle, for he had learned that in coming to St Ulric's he had only exchanged one ministry for another. The new ministry may be very differently structured, with colleagues engaged in other kinds of activity. Yet, as in his parish, so in St Ulric's he was sharing in the faith-life of a community in which each had their own place in a common task. As one of the pastoral theologians, he had not only his own particular responsibility but also the task of helping to draw out the gospel word for the life of the college and for each challenging situation as it arose.

This had two significant expressions. With colleagues, junior and senior, there were the issues that faced the whole community as it lived together. In this Charles knew and gladly accepted that he was but one of a company, where formal leadership lay with the Principal. Nevertheless, he recognized that his own designated position must include such contribution as was reasonable to the spiritual development of the college. So he saw clearly the value of the staff–student Common Room committee and was happy to encourage various aspects of communal life, as well as to be available for pastoral conversation.

More formally, in his work and the work of his team with the students, his role as practical theologian was crucial. In the first instance it gave a focus to the model of the practical theologian in ministry. All the practical field work, classroom learning and skills acquisition – not only in practical theology but from the other theological and human science classes – all this was to enable the students to become familiar with and gain confidence in the process of theological reflection. For the heart of ministry is to facilitate others, both in the group setting and individually, in the pilgrimage of faith. Whatever the necessary technical resources needed for the execution of those special tasks that fall to the ministry, from biblical exegesis to management, they are all present in the people of God, so that together they can live more faithfully and more obediently.

At the same time, the heart of preparation for ministry can only truly lie in exploring the path for oneself, growing in the gospel by participating in a living community of faith. This will largely happen in and through the formal processes of training, for it is impossible to reflect on pastoral cases or to discuss issues of society or faith without being personally affected. But there also has to be opportunity for self-awareness and personal growth which is integrated into an enlarging spirituality. This comes from corporate discipline and worship and those points of personal encounter both formal – in tutorial contact or prayer group – and informal – over coffee or agonizing into the small hours over some issue or another.

At this point, however, it must now be clear that being a practical theologian is not simply being the one appointed to a designated office or bound by formal academic demands. Rather it is being at the heart of ministry. It is the pastor in the community, in and with the congregation or in any similar setting, who is the true practical theologian; for practical theology finds its proper function precisely at that point where the people of God seek to discern the presence of God in the world and to live by faithful obedience. The ordained minister is the symbolic representative of this task. Within the Christian community he or she enables the people, together and personally, to open themselves to their calling in Christ, in Word and sacrament, in pastoral care and occasional office, and no less importantly in group discussion, acts of service, shared experience and neighbourly conversation. Beyond, in the wider community, the minister is inevitably the representative Christian presence in word and deed, through the structures of local society and in its communal relationships.

This has been expressed forcefully by John de Gruchy.

> The pastoral and prophetic responsibility of the ordained min-
> istry, the 'cure of souls' and the proclamation of the Word of
> God derive from the calling to enable the people to know, trust
> and obey God in Jesus Christ. This requires relating the Chris-
> tian faith to contemporary situations, a communicative task
> best described as practical theology. The model of the ordained
> minister as practical theologian transcends the historic division
> (priest and minister). These distinctive emphases remain but
> priest and prophet find their community in providing direction
> to the community of faith engaged in mission in the world.[7]

Thus here too the assigned tasks expected of the ministry may give shape and content to ministerial action in such areas as worship, administration, pastoral care and community action; but these cannot be understood as being a sole prerogative, the heart of one's identity. They are there as service to the whole Christian body so that the community, in all its parts, may be indeed a sign of Word and sacrament, witness and service in obedience to the call of the Kingdom. The office of ministry is always representa-tive – a mark and sign of that which is true for the whole. It seemed to Charles that if he had one thing to say to his colleagues at the conference for which he was preparing, this was it.

What then are the marks of the practical theologian? First, perhaps the greatest gift that the practical theologian brings is a greater awareness of the wisdom of the tradition. This is the point of all that academic study during training (whether successful or not): to be able to help others handle the Bible, to grow in understanding and to be open to greater possibilities. In classical theological parlance, the minister represents the wider Church in the local situation. However, this is not merely to instruct but also to participate in the reality of the local tradition, as it falteringly but creatively searches out its own commitment and understanding. For the minister is also, with others, representative of local and contingent realities in the councils of the wider Church.

Secondly, the minister is the representative Christian, in two senses: as the public presence of the Church's concern, whether on a school board or at a hospital bedside, as the public disciple, living close to the Lord and mediating his presence. Such a calling can become intolerable but cannot be escaped. One of the interesting themes to emerge in recent years has been the emphasis on ministry as presence. The priest or minister represents the possibility of believing in the reality of the alternative vision that faith proposes: someone who is freed from the pressures of the world's madness to live at a different pace, to another tune. Terry Holmes points to the same kind of concern when he suggests that the minister is a kind of shaman or holy person who carries the expectations of the presence of God for those around.[8] This should not be seen simply as a burden, a weight to be carried, piled on with others' expectations. It is in fact the form of discovery of the gospel: of working with one's own reality in the context of where we are placed, and there finding forgiveness and grace, renewal and patience, support and encouragement, failure and success, all of which are the stuff of Christian obedience. The glory of the high calling to ministry is to share personally in the pursuit of the fullness of Christ that is the destiny of the whole Church.

Thirdly, the minister usually presides at the table. This is most clearly seen at the Eucharist, but the table of the Lord must not be separated from other shared meals, such as the Harvest Supper, or the boardroom table around which the Church Council sits. The whole community is gathered in each place to share in the common life and to bring all its gifts, opportunities and needs, so that in the Holy Spirit, together and as each is called, they may serve Christ in the world. It is the task of creating the common life. John de Gruchy again points to this:

The real theological task is . . . to enable the community of faith critically to understand the faith and to express answers to the questions: Who is God? Where is God to be found today and what does this God require of us here and now? The academic theologian may well provide resources for answering these questions. But it is the practical theologian within the community of faith who has to help the community day by day and week by week discover the answers in relation to the praxis and witness of the Church in the world and so help it find the direction which enables it to be faithful to its task.[9]

The whole people of God

That, thought Charles, is as good an outline of three points as will be possible. But we ought to go further. As a practical theologian the minister is exercising a particular ministry on behalf of the whole community. In this there are special tasks and responsibilities. But it is fundamentally the ministry of the whole people of God. Therefore it can also be said that the practice of practical theology is the calling of all and each member of the Body of Christ.

In the first instance the processes of discernment, reflection and commitment are embedded in and arise out of the church life of the people. It is a corporate activity, weaving itself into the living tradition of the community, expressed in a myriad of ways as well as in the deliberate and formal shared enterprise. Charles remembered with joy many conversations out of which came real wisdom. The gathering in worship, fellowship, reflection and deliberation is the pulse of theological reflection. Secondly, there will be those who, within the structures of the Church or beyond it, will be recognized as having a ministry, participating in the process of practical theology through their skills, experience or wisdom. Again Charles thought of people he knew, as much in the community as in the Church, who were clearly part of this whole process of service and witness. Such people are necessary alongside the ordained ministry. Practical theology is a shared activity in which insights and visions emerge from a diversity of sources. There is no monopoly of wisdom or spiritual insight. Thirdly, and most importantly, however, all Christians in their daily lives engage in practical theology, for each has to live as a disciple in the actual circumstances and demands of life. In a proper way,

this is inevitably personal. So the fellowship of worship and reflection, and the pastoral care that is either one-to-one or in the
group, is the foundation of the Church in the home, the work-
place, along the street or in leisure activity. In the particularity of
each situation there is also the shared ministry of living the
gospel.

Charles recognized that such a vision was very difficult to
sustain. There were many external pressures that would make a
more secure and defined role attractive. In the congregation it is
so easy to allow legitimate tasks to become exclusive responsibilities, and the necessary authority of office to become the basis of
separate and sacralized identity. People have their own perception
as to what the minister is there to do, and can let respect for the
ministry of Word and sacrament slip into something near dependency. And this is perhaps even more true of many people in the
wider community who turn to the Church for rites of passage and
occasional offices, looking for the correct responses from the
religious officiant. Collusion in all this is natural and tempting.
Everyone needs to have recognition and standing, some ordered
place that structures and gives meaning to existence. Nor are the
temptations very different in the academic setting. It is necessary
to have a recognized field within the overall task. The expectation
is to have a specialization for teaching and research. In neither
context is it easy to live up to Sydney Evans' image of the true
amateur, not lacking in skill and commitment, but free to be and
to respond as the need demands, losing one's identity for the sake
of the common cause.[10]

At the same time Charles recognized all the allies he had met
on the way. Like Bunyan's Pilgrim, he too had found support and
instruction, companionship and generosity from so many. These
were and are the real practical theologians in whose company
Charles felt called to serve. They included people from his now
increasingly distant past, grandparents, school chaplains, teachers; those who had ministered to him in his own ministry in their
homes and workplaces, in times of sorrow and joy, of decision and
anxiety. He was especially grateful for the experience of setting up
a counselling centre in the country town where he had been vicar.
This, perhaps more than anything, had begun that shift in his own
perspective and practice from offering a service on the basis of
an expertise and authority, to working alongside people from a
position of partnership. In the counselling room it becomes abun-

dantly clear that the focus is on the client, to enable them, out of the freedom of their own self-awareness, to take their own decisions and to appropriate for themselves the necessary resources, whether from within or from those around or from the gospel itself, in order to live more creatively within the limits of their own possibilities. It was not easy, however, to abdicate power, to become the servant.

This process had been gladly confirmed and strengthened through his colleagues in St Ulric's. Margaret consistently held up the model of community development, of working with people in their shared task, as the basis for ministry both within and beyond the congregation. In the end, true understanding and good practice are only possible if they are appropriated and owned, becoming part of the fabric of the community. This chimed in well with the attitudes he found informing the work of training lay leadership at Damian Hall, the Catholic centre also associated with the University. Ministry is the work of the whole people of God in which there are many tasks which are shared out and done for the good of the whole. The work of the practical theologian is to participate in and be a catalyst for the common life of the whole Christian community.

For these reasons it was good to take to heart the warning given by St Augustine found embedded in the Vatican II document *Lumen Gentium*:

> As the laity, through the divine choices, have Christ as their brother, who, though Lord of all, came not to be served but to serve, they also have as brothers those in the sacred ministry. As St Augustine very beautifully puts it: 'When I am frightened by what I am to you, then I am consoled by what I am with you. To you I am bishop, with you I am a Christian. The first is an office, the second a grace; the first a danger, the second salvation.'[11]

Charles found such a process of reflection tiring and yet challenging. He was glad he had done it, for it had helped him to clarify a great deal that had as yet only been buzzing round his mind. Indeed he felt a sense of elation, of having completed a stage of his own development. So, with more than enough to occupy the slot he had been given, he decided to approach his talk as a form of celebration and an invitation to his colleagues in the diocese. For they were not to be there just to hear about theology, but to be helped to see that they are actually the true theologians – servants of the servants of God.

Notes

1 Amirtham, Samuel and Pobee, John S. (eds), *Theology by the People* (WCC 1986), pp. 128–9.
2 The practical theologian, therefore, in John V. Taylor's terminology, is the theologian of the Holy Spirit, the one who points to and participates in the creative invisibility of the God who holds all things together. See his *Go-Between God* (SCM 1972).
3 Faber, Hije, *Pastoral Care in the Modern Hospital* (SCM 1971).
4 Industrial Mission is not well documented publicly, though there is a considerable occasional literature. Two older books give contrasting introductions to I.M. work: Taylor, Richard, *Christians in an Industrial Society* (SCM 1961); and Velten, George, *Mission in Industrial France* (SCM 1962). Also the report, *Industrial Mission – an Appraisal* (BSR 1988).
5 In Ballard, Paul H., *The Foundations of Pastoral Studies and Practical Theology* (University College, Cardiff 1986), p. 95.
6 Various aspects of this process will be taken up in Part II.
7 De Gruchy, John, *Theology and Ministry in Context and Crisis* (Harper and Row 1966), p. 25.
8 Holmes, U.T., *The Priest in Community* (Seabury 1978), pp. 68–95.
9 De Gruchy, op. cit., p. 55.
10 From a personal conversation. Sydney Evans was formerly Dean of King's College, London and subsequently Dean of Salisbury.
11 Flannery, Austin, ed.: *Vatican Council II – The Conciliar and Postconciliar Documents* (Fowler Wright 1981), para. 33.

Chapter 4

Theory and practice

At the heart of all theology there lies a particular set of crucial theoretical yet practical issues. What is the relation between the specific theological activity of describing the nature and content of the Christian faith, and what Christians actually do in their lives? How do we get from words to action, from proclamation to pastoral care? That is: what is the relation between theory, ideas and doctrine, on the one hand, and the practical action which expresses that belief on the other? Such questions clearly lie at the centre of practical theology's concerns, for it is there, in the formal sense, that they are explicitly brought to the surface.

In some form or other the practical theologian always has to face the demand of acting well in the light of the gospel. But, as always, this is only an expression of the fundamental everyday task of every Christian believer. This means that what may appear to be a highly technical and abstract philosophical discussion, is in fact directly relevant to the immediate situation of each Christian, and certainly to the minister as one who leads the Christian community in its life together and in its involvement in society. How we understand the relation between theory and practice shapes the way we act as Christians.

This was the issue facing Kate, both practically and theoretically. Kate had come to Stoke Chewsbury as a Team Vicar in one of the two groups of Anglican parishes based on the small market town some twenty miles from the university city that dominated the region. For Kate, at this point in her career, two things were proving very worthwhile. First, she had enrolled on a course with the local Theology Department in the university. This was forcing her to deepen her theological resources; but, most helpfully, it required her to do her reading in relation to her actual pastoral situation. This meant that Kate was continually reflecting on her experience in the light of what she had learned and was having to test and explore what she had learned in the light of the reality of her daily work. It was not easy; indeed it was hard work, stretching her powers of imagination and creativity. Yet it was all worthwhile.

Secondly, however, Kate had also discovered the value of the monthly clergy meeting in the town. Not only were they all regularly present, the Catholic priest together with the Pentecostal and Baptist pastors, the Methodist and United Reformed ministers and the four Anglican clergy; but there had grown up over the years a strength of fellowship, support and mutuality that enabled them to share at a deep level. One of its values, therefore, was being able to bring to the group pastoral concerns with which help was needed. So it was not unusual when Kate introduced her anxiety about Jayne and her daughter Effie. They all understood that for Kate there were two levels of agenda: her genuine concern for Jayne and her use of this situation to reflect on the nature of theological method (which is what makes it of interest to us).[1]

Jayne had separated from her husband, Bob, because she had eventually rebelled at his physical abuse of herself and sexual abuse of Effie who was now fourteen. Jayne and Effie moved into one of the old workers' cottages between St Oswald's, where Kate ministered, and the old mill. This was cheap enough to allow Jayne to support them both by taking up nursery teaching again in the private school that used the church halls during the week. It was there that Kate met Jayne, and gradually both mother and daughter had been drawn into the edges of parish life, occasionally attending worship, doing the odd job or joining in some of the social events. But things were becoming complicated.

Chris, a lifelong friend, had been a tower of strength over the traumatic period. He now wanted to move in with Jayne, though he was not pressing his point. But the very possibility was threatening to trigger off all kinds of repercussions. The settlement with Bob was proving very difficult and any move by Jayne might set all that back, let alone produce what could well be a violent reaction. Effie was clearly not happy and had, indeed, had problems at school. There were suspicions of drug abuse as well as some truancy. Moreover, in talking things over with Kate, Jayne revealed that she was herself an abused child and was terrified of going through the whole process again. So low was her estimation of herself that what would appear to be an affirmation of her through Chris's care was seen as yet another threat.

When Kate brought this case to the group, the conversation was helpfully wide-ranging. They shared information about the law and the role of the Social Services, and where Jayne could find affordable counselling out of town to help her in her own self-discovery. They discussed the way they, and especially Kate, could offer pastoral care to both Jayne and Effie, and what the church community could do. They looked at the issues raised by Chris and Bob. They asked what could be done creatively in relation to the youth of the town. All this was of considerable practical help to Kate: new information, ideas about personal support and steps to take as she tried to get alongside both Jayne and Effie. But Kate was also taking extensive notes on the meeting and it was these that formed the material for her reflection on theological method. So when she got home that evening, Kate began to work out how each of her colleagues ticked as those who had the task of offering pastoral care in the midst of complex events.

As she did this, to her surprise, Kate began to discern a four-fold pattern – similar to one that she had already begun to discern in the literature she was reading. At the same time the 'fault-lines' did not by any means run along denominational or other obvious boundaries but cut across expected divisions. It was not that a series of watertight compartments appeared, pigeon holes into which to slot people. Rather there were some clear emphases which overlapped or allied themselves with each other. Yet, even in so small a group, these categories could be reasonably clearly discerned. Kate could easily imagine that a larger sample would allow for greater differentiation and precision and that the same models would be found in other areas of discourse, like education or technology.

Practice arises from theory

The first of these approaches was shared by Huw, the Baptist pastor, and Fr Richard, the Anglo-Catholic vicar of St Bridget's, the parish at the other end of town. Not surprisingly, Huw was anxious to establish the biblical principles that should inform Kate's actions. Her task was to set out clearly 'what the Bible says' and to urge Jayne to live in conformity with this teaching. This was tolerably clear in the area of Chris and Jayne's relationship but was equally applicable, it was being suggested, to other issues, such as the need to exercise forgiveness or the possibility of overcoming fear. Richard's way looked slightly different, yet in reality was the same. For him it was a matter of discovering what the Church teaches. The pastoral task is to guide people along the path of traditional holiness. The sacramental framework would, slowly but surely, enable Jayne to find the grace of divine forgiveness and the strength to discover her path through the maze of her life's circumstances. The obvious means of grace would be the confessional and the Eucharist.

Kate recognized here – though almost certainly Huw and Richard would have found it surprising – an approach which owes its strength to Enlightenment rationalism and which has profoundly influenced the way theology has been understood and used. Both Huw and Richard started with a given truth, an axiomatic point of reference, from which the consequences are deduced. Once the fundamental ground has been established, from it will flow, logically, all that is needed. So, find the right law of natural science or of society and it is possible to predict the movements of the stars or the behaviour of the markets. For Huw, even though he was no fundamentalist, the Bible was the starting point, for through it we are given the pattern of God's revelation. In modern Protestant theology this has been the Barthian tradition. The pastoral task is to mediate the Word of God. For Richard the *magisterium* of the Church, its teaching authority, preserves the authentic voice of the gospel and, by careful argument from precedent, the priest discerns how it should be applied in particular instances.

Clearly, such a position corresponds to a very real experience. The Christian gospel does indeed come as grace, as something given which does not depend on our effort or receptivity. God comes to us in the reality of Christ and reaches out to us in the means of grace. Our task and joy is to respond to the gift, freedom and renewal that is offered. We hear the gospel as God's good will towards fallen but much-loved creatures. Was it not this that had already drawn Jayne into the congregation, given her hope and drawn her to seek pastoral help? Where else should she turn? If the gospel gives life, then it sets its own standards, expectations and demands. Christ has been given to us and he stands in the midst with us and for us.

If that was the 'deductive way', Kate also discerned in her

colleagues an 'inductive way'. It would appear that these are opposed to one another. At one level that is true. The deductive way starts with a given truth from which all is deduced; whereas the inductive way starts with the evidence and then, by induction, arrives at a conclusion. Yet they are not actually so far apart. The 'inductive' claims to discover the underlying pattern from empirical observation, but then it is used deductively. Both want to have their theory right before asking: what do I do?

James, the senior circuit Methodist minister, was like that. Theology for him was really a matter of establishing the truth of the faith. The task of natural or fundamental theology is to argue the foundations of faith in philosophical and historical terms. So we investigate the possibility of belief in God and how God relates to the world. We also ask what it is reasonable to believe about Jesus, and whether the history of Christianity has compromised the great claims it makes. We are asked, in the biblical phrase, to 'give account for the hope that is in us' (1 Pet. 3.15). Thus James was willing to argue that some of the expectations that Jayne had as to what Christians are meant to teach, are not in fact so unchangingly inscribed on tablets of stone.

The classic exponent of this approach was Schleiermacher. He could defend theology as an academic subject in that theology's primary task was to establish the reasonableness of Christianity. Although he saw theology not as a pure science but as a practical science like law and medicine, its practice had to be based on soundly and critically established principles arrived at in the market place of ideas. The weakness of such a position is that there is no necessary connection between theory and practice. Theory becomes an end in itself, a search that is never completed, always subject to revision. Meanwhile practitioners must to some extent assume the theory. That is, while the academics are still arguing, the practitioner has to get on with the job – even if based on indifferent or antiquated theory. Thus a gap may open up between the two: the theoretician sceptical of the practitioner's inadequate understanding and the practitioner indifferent to the abstractions of theory. This is a gap frequently encountered: between theologian and pastor, or priest and congregation. Jayne and Effie may not have needed to go through all the debate, but they were in fact affected by it.

The way of critical correlation

It was Brian, Kate's rector, who positioned himself in the gap
between what he called 'the language of Zion' and the other
voices to be heard in her conversations with Jayne and Effie. The
pastoral relationship gave Kate no automatic right to be heard
and she only had the authority that she could secure through the
effectiveness of her presence. Meanwhile, there were many others
involved in the situation, from professional helpers to friends and
neighbours. What the gospel had to offer had to make its own way
in the open forum of public debate.

According to Brian, the Christian perspective had to be seen as
a reasonable and attractive possibility alongside alternatives. In
the end Jayne and Effie were having to make their own way
through the jungle of life, selecting their own allies, making their
own judgements. So, while Kate reckoned she had a good relationship with Effie, she recognized that she was outside the world
of a modern teenager. The pressures on Effie were considerable:
to join the gang, experiment with drugs, to flout authority. Her
adult world had let her down badly and now mum was threatening to dump her again for a man. And is there any future anyway?
Jayne too had good well-meaning neighbours and colleagues at
work. Heaven knows what they said, let alone those closely
involved. Then there were the doctor and the counsellor Jayne was
seeing, and the solicitors involved in the custody and divorce
proceedings.

Kate recognized that she too was part of this debate, because
faith does not divorce us from society. It is necessary to live in the
community, sharing the responsibility and using the professional
and other services that enable us all to function. So there is a
constant dialogue between the perspectives that seem to be
demanded by faith and those that impinge on us from elsewhere.
That is, we have to correlate the wisdom of the Christian tradition
with the insights and understandings that normally guide our
everyday activities and practical decisions. It was this public
demand that Brian was anxious to underline. In pastoral care the
clergy will be found working alongside others, offering a specialized ministry but also sharing with others in the search for the
most effective practical insights and action in this situation. This
is the point that Don Browning has been constantly making as the
fundamental cornerstone of practical theology: practical theology

must be seen to be speaking realistically to people in their actual situations and to be part of the public ethical process.

Kate further realized that this dialectical process between the Christian faith and other information and ideas, was not only external to the Christian community, part of her task as a representative of the Church through its official ministry; it was also internal to the life of the Church, because every Christian and each community of faith has to live according to the light of the gospel in an ever-changing world. So, for example, the Christian professionals are always challenged to bring together their faith and their professional world view; or the local Church has to ask what should be its response to the social assumptions about family, divorce, personal relations, or AIDS, as they impinge on its own life and the community around. Within the household of faith, however, the process will be more explicit, for there the tradition of Scripture, the wisdom of the saints and the liturgy will be drawn on as authoritative sources; but they still have to be brought into creative dialogue with the discoveries made in the contemporary world.

In this, Kate was grateful for some remarks – albeit from very different points of view – from Sarah, her United Reformed colleague and Steve, the curate at St Bridget's. Sarah suggested drawing parallels between pastoral care and writing a sermon. The two are linked, she said, because liturgical preaching is done within a living community. The pastor is aware on the one hand of the gospel that has to be proclaimed and is found primarily in the lectionary passages and the seasons of the Christian year, but also in teaching material, books, art, music, and the generally received tradition. On the other hand the pastor is aware of the life of the community, its hopes and fears, its wider context, and individuals and families within and around it. The point of the sermon is to create the place where the living Word can be heard as the two are brought together. We who are being changed, moulded and formed under the pressures, opportunities and joys of our time, ask the tradition to give of its wisdom so that we may understand who we are and what we can believe and what we must do as Christ's people. As Sarah, who was the group's biblical scholar, put it: The big word for this is hermeneutics; the easier one is dialogue – dialogue between the Christian tradition and human experience.

She pointed out that biblical interpretation can be seen as a kind of conversation with the text and, at the same time, with the people with whom we are involved. The pastor is the interpreter, trying to suss out what is going on and how to see where there are signs of the gospel. At a theoretical level this whole approach will be a critical correlation between theology and the social sciences, together illuminating the human condition. This method of 'critical correlation' has become central to much recent practical theology, not least in North America, developing a theme found in Paul Tillich and elaborated in more recent hermeneutical theology such as that of David Tracy. In practice it will more often be done piecemeal – in discussion groups, in worship, in pastoral conversation, or chance encounter. Yet the sermon is perhaps the right focal image, for it is in the liturgy that the fellowship of faith identifies itself around Word and sacrament, and listens with expectation as it offers itself in service to God in the world.

Steve, however, spoke about contemplative prayer and meditation. Once again there is the sense of deliberate detachment, of taking time to reflect on and to become aware of the deeper dimensions of existence. The person engaged in prayer stands back in order to see the reality of God, of the world, and of ourselves. But disengagement is not renunciation; rather a deeper commitment to reality as it is. We do not leave the world, but see the world in God, the God and Father of our Lord Jesus Christ.

Prayer finds, in and through the concrete reality, the living presence of God. It is essentially sacramental in form, recognizing the spiritual dimension which is always present in the material and historical. One of the classic approaches to meditation is to envisage a Gospel scene and then to enter into it, be caught up in it and to discover Christ's word to us.[2] It is also possible to take others there with us in our mind's eye. So Kate could carry Effie and Jayne into the presence of Christ, or with Jairus call for help for the child, or wonder how Jayne can touch the hem of his robe. But Kate could start at the other end too and invite Christ into that workman's cottage which is the centre of Jayne and Effie's life, to meet them there, as well as to touch the lives of everyone else who goes in and out. As she does this perhaps new themes and possibilities may emerge, or she may discover what Christ's loving embrace is for these people as he watches and bears with them. Such a model is not confined to private prayer but could be used by groups, in prayer and discussion. Indeed, thought Kate, perhaps this had been what was happening in the group as it had helped her to understand Jayne and Effie better and had given her new personal tasks and opportunities.

Understanding on the basis of experience

It was Bill, the younger Methodist minister, who appeared to be the odd one out. His concern seemed to push theological issues to one side and, first of all, to analyse more clearly Jayne's situation and to set it in a wider context. He noted that Jayne was in a situation that appeared increasingly typical in today's society: family breakdown, one-parent families, violence, poverty and the cycle of deprivation. Jayne and Effie had in fact done quite well despite having so much stacked against them. He could envisage Effie sliding into prostitution or heavy drugs. Bill was well appreciative of the job Kate was doing but it was equally important for him to ask what this meant concerning the dynamics and structures of society and what it meant in a town like theirs, with its collapsing agriculturally based community, its new commuting middle class and the small but typical low income housing estates on the fringe.

There may not be much that the churches of Stoke Chewsbury could do but that does not mean nothing could happen. It was still necessary not only to work with individuals but to set up points of active resistance and to offer glimpses of an alternative mode of human existence. That was precisely what Bill was trying to do in the little Methodist country chapel which had been swallowed up when the council estate was built. There was now a community centre which provided a focus for local action and development and a place of trust where everyone could work for themselves and their common life. At the same time Bill had initiated the small part-time industrial mission programme in association with the regional industrial mission team through the local council of churches. Kate herself, and two or three others, were finding themselves involved in the commercial, industrial and trading activities of the town, and working with the local authorities in education, health and local government.

As she analysed her notes Kate realized that it was not that Bill was not interested in theology, but that he located it in a different place. It brought back memories of her theological college and her encounters with liberation theology, which had then seemed set at a considerable distance in Latin America. Their Christian understanding arose from their experience of dire poverty and political oppression but was suspect for many because it seemed tainted with Marxism. In any case, Marxism seemed to be old hat since the collapse of the Berlin Wall. Yet was it really so remote? Kate had become increasingly aware of parallel interests in this country. There were the radical evangelicals from whom she had learned so much, exemplified by David Sheppard's *Bias to the Poor.*[3] There were some feminist theologians offering some stringent analyses of society. Then there was the considerable furore caused by *Faith in the City.*[4] And there was much to learn from industrial mission itself.

In their monthly meetings Bill constantly seemed to strike two notes. The first was that his primary theological reality was the Kingdom of God. To speak of the Kingdom points to the future when the broken, damaged and oppressed will find justice, peace and joy. But the Kingdom is also a present reality, struggling to find expression and to shape the lives of people and community. We are called to serve the Kingdom not only where faith is found but wherever love, truth, justice and peace are demonstrated in shared lives and human structures. Thus we can stumble over the Kingdom in the most unlikely places: in the slums of the city, in the loyalty and love of the seemingly useless, in the gift of dedicated care, or in the supportive community. It is the Church's task to witness to the Kingdom and to be in the struggle for its establishment.

This pointed to Bill's second concern. The starting point, he said, is at the bottom, with the poor and oppressed, the damaged and the handicapped. That is where the gospel is found. In the words of the Magnificat, God 'has put down the mighty from their thrones, and exalted those of low degree' (Luke 1.52). It is a revolutionary but not necessarily violent idea that will turn the world upside down. The Lord is the one who brings his people out of bondage (Exod. 20.2).

What Bill was insistent upon was that Christian truth is found precisely in committed action. Theory and practice are dialectically locked together, for theory or understanding arises out of action, and action relates to reflection on interpreted action. Truth is found in doing, and truth is always something done. Faith becomes real in the doing. This is the heart of the Marxist notion of 'praxis' that is so central to liberation theology. As a result, theology starts where God is to be found, in the concrete reality of the immediate situation. So theology starts with analysis, with understanding how things actually are, so that the possibilities of the Kingdom can then be discerned. This was why Bill insisted on looking at Jayne's situation in the round, as part of society's general state, as well as in terms of her particular situation. Jayne's dilemma was part of the way the Kingdom is found in Stoke Chewsbury. As a result of Bill's intervention some action was taken: to recruit for Relate's local educational programme, and the Council of Churches initiative in schools was reaffirmed. Perhaps thereby a little pressure could be taken off some of those places where the shoe pinched for Jayne and Effie and for many others. Kate was glad to be reminded of the liberationist dictum: 'seeing analytically, judging theologically, and acting pastorally, three phases in one commitment in faith'.

The praxis model may counter the threat of abstract intellectualism, of belief coming before practice; but, Kate wondered, was it not still true that there has to be a prior commitment to truth, a truth that has to be argued for? Why is the option for the poor the correct starting point? Does it not have to be accepted in faith? In any case, is it right to have such a single-minded perspective? Could we not be narrowing the gospel, discarding other dimensions of the tradition? For all its dangers, is it not necessary to affirm both the priority of God in Christ as well as that faith is only real in action?

The community of meaning

Perhaps Kate's strangest discovery was to experience how close Liam, the Catholic priest, and Peter, the Pentecostal minister, were to each other, despite all the apparent differences between them in language and practice. Both of them assumed that what would help Jayne and Effie most was a strong, accepting, supportive community that could provide them with a sense of belonging to a family. In such a context they could explore the richness of the gospel while being given status and dignity, freedom and forgiveness, renewal and strength. The task of the Church is to be the community of faith in which the life of Christ is embodied as light in the world, a place of new possibilities.

Liam, of course, saw this in terms that have become familiar since the Second Vatican Council. The Church is the pilgrim people of God, scattered across the world but identifiable in each

place. The Church is the sacrament of salvation, a sign in the
world of God's present and transforming love. Thus there is a new
sense of belonging to the Christian community with its own
forms of life and experience. This has undergirded the liturgical
reforms of recent years in the Catholic Church that have made
the worship more participatory and corporate in nature. The cat-
echetical models used these days emphasize the sense of travelling
together, of sharing stories, of growing closer to each other as we
grow closer to Christ. This was all remarkably similar to Peter's
insistence that the Church should be an alternative society in the
midst of the world. He admitted that this can be interpreted in
narrowly sectarian ways but pointed to other expressions of the
tradition such as is found among some Mennonites such as John
Yoder and Jim Wallis.[5] In many churches the need for a sense of
distinctiveness in an increasingly pluralistic and secular society
has been recognized.

Two further points also emerged. The first is that Christian
ethical perspectives and demands make much more sense as the
description of the way of life within the community of faith. They
are, on this view, patterns into which one is increasingly drawn.
Moreover, the basis for ethical behaviour is less one of command,
still less of benefit, but of habit and virtue, a theme that Kate recognized as running through much ethical discourse from classical
theism to contemporary attempts, such as by Alasdair MacIntyre,
to re-establish the ethics of virtue.[6] The ethical task is to fill out
that to which we have been called in Christ and for which we are
being formed by the Spirit. The aim of Christian nurture at every
level is to produce a Christlike quality of character.

Secondly, ethics and theology come close together, for the
theological task is not divorced from the whole life of faith, but
serves it. That is, theology is one of the activities which, with
prayer and sacrament and faithful action, forms the Christian
character. Learning about God and his ways is undertaken in
order to know God in himself. It is here that the distinction
between theory and practice disappears, for both are part of the
service of God: the one to contemplate the mystery of the divine
grace, the other to express that grace in and through our whole
being. Through both, we are being directed to one end and suf-
fused by the divine grace so that the glory of God is the nature of
our reality. It becomes a 'habitus', a part of our nature; what the
Eastern theologians call 'divinization'.

Kate realized that she, let alone Jayne and Effie, had hardly begun on this journey. In any case it is a lifelong process of ever deepening wisdom and widening vision. Yet each of them had really taken some steps along the road. The question was how she, Jayne and Effie and all the others in the congregation could be further and further drawn into the mysteries of Christ so that 'we all attain to the unity of the faith and the knowledge of the Son of God, to mature humanity, to the measure of the stature of the fullness of Christ' (Eph. 4.13). Yet the danger noted by Brian (see pp. 50–51) still remains: that the separation between the Church and the world may be such a divide that they become remote from each other – unable to communicate or relate.

Conclusion

From her notes Kate believed she had drawn out four fundamental models concerning the relation between theory and practice. She had also noted some of the strengths and weaknesses of each position. But how were they to be related together? Were they essentially incompatible, strictly alternatives? In fact, however, it would seem that each tended to correspond to a significant Christian affirmation and therefore commanded its own attention and respect.

(i) That practice is applied theory points to the reality of God's grace and initiative in creation and salvation, to which we respond in faith. (The applied theory model.)

(ii) That Christian living comes out of a dialogue between the tradition and contemporary reality, not least by public discourse (the critical correlation/hermeneutical model), stresses the belief that 'all truth is God's truth' and that we are on a continuous exploration into truth.

(iii) That theory is a reflection on practice and arises from committed action (the praxis model) underlines that faith is essentially a transformative activity, serving the manifestation of the Kingdom.

(iv) That truth is found in the community of shared meaning and that it is appropriated by a process of growth into wisdom (the habitus/virtue model) takes seriously the need to accept the distinctiveness of faith, and of the Church as a sign of renewal in the world.

Trouble would seem to arise when one or other model is seen as the only model, distorting and restricting theological activity. It is better to see each as a possible entry point into a complex and continuous process; and that each needs to be corrected and challenged by the other. So Jayne and Effie are indeed being confronted with the gospel, which comes as gracious demand; but at the same time the pastoral concern is with them as real people, set in an actual context, facing real problems. It is there that the gospel imperative and gift has to be found. Part of this is to find refuge and strength in the supportive community, learning its values and ways; yet pastoral care has to help them see their way forward in daily life in the light of the best advice and help they can find.

Notes

1   In this chapter extensive bibliographical and theological references are not given as they can be found in Chapter 5.
2   This is at the heart of the Ignatian method but can be found in other systems. See, e.g. Gordon Wakefield (ed.), *Dictionary of Christian Spirituality* (SCM 1982).
3   Sheppard, David, *Bias to the Poor* (Hodder and Stoughton 1983).
4   Church House Publishing 1985.
5   The Mennonites originate from a sixteenth-century Dutch Anabaptist group founded by Meno Simons. Like some similar groups they were pacifist and have a strong community tradition, exemplified today in the Sojourners in Washington DC, but they, unlike some exclusive groups, have a strong commitment to witnessing in contemporary society.
6   MacIntyre, Alasdair, *After Virtue* (Duckworth 1981).

Chapter 5

Models for practical theology

If we go back with Kate from her meeting with her colleagues in town and into her study, we can follow her into the next step of her voyage of discovery. Kate recognizes that there are several things that she will have to do in a practical way to follow up the discussion; but she also has another obligation. As part of her course at the university Kate has to prepare a paper for a seminar. She has been asked to reflect on how her experience related to, and is helped by, the differing models of practical theology, patterns she has already begun to discern in the reactions of her colleagues. What kind of framework should she adopt? In order to do this she has to explore the literature and see if there emerges a typology or range of models which are commonly used in doing practical theology.

This chapter, then, is still concerned with the foundations of practical theology. It is an attempt to set out in a more formal way the important models that inform various expressions of practical theology. It is also intended to be an introduction to some of the primary literature about the practice of practical theology. The hope is that this will provide an accessible introduction and launching pad for those who wish to come to grips with the complexities of the field in greater depth and which can become a fascinating journey of exploration. Others, however, may wish to skip this bit (for the time being) and come back to it later, though material in later chapters relates clearly to what is set out here.

Four models are suggested. They should not, however, be regarded as disparate or mutually exclusive. Rather they should be regarded as strands which are often woven together and affect each other. It may be possible to discern broad types but it is very

hard to characterize particular individual approaches to situations
with any absolute finality. Yet such a typology is useful. It provides
a conceptual framework, a kind of grid, that helps us map the field
with greater clarity.

Practical theology as applied theory

The distinction between theoretical or pure science, and applied
science or technology is one that is widely assumed and taken for
granted. The pure scientist, it is thought, disinterestedly searches
for truth, pushing back the frontiers of human knowledge. The
technologist, however, is seen as primarily interested in seeking
new applications or solving problems, applying the relevant
theory to practical ends; as the electrical goods advert has it: 'the
appliance of science'.

This is, in fact, a model that comes out of the Enlightenment,[1]
or Age of Reason, during which the foundations of modern
science and society were laid. One of the key tenets of Enlightenment thinking is that knowledge and truth give power and
wisdom. Human well-being will be based on a knowledge of the
laws of the universe, including human behaviour, and on learning
to conform to or use them.

In practical theology this model can be found in two forms.
First it is possible to talk of applying the results of the social sciences to the pastoral situation. The pastor turns to a suitable body
of teaching to use as a tool. So, for instance, Rogerian counselling
theory and skills are taken up as the foundation of pastoral
methodology. The danger is that the social or psychological
theory may dictate the direction and patterns of pastoral practice.
This will be taken up again in Chapter 8 when we examine the
way different disciplines relate to and support each other.

Secondly, there is also a version of the model of applied theory
that has been widely accepted in relation to theology itself. The
point of authority and truth has first to be established, but now
instead of it being the relevant social or psychological theory, it is
theology which takes the lead. This may be the Bible as sufficient
in faith and morals; or the teaching authority of the Church; or
even, in more liberal circles, natural theology established by
reason. But once accepted, appropriate actions and obligations
are deduced on the basis of its authority. Christians are expected
to obey the commands of God, however mediated. The task of

discipleship is obedience. Karl Barth called Friedrich Schleiermacher (1768–1834) 'the father of modern theology'. It was
Schleiermacher who gave classic expression to this approach to
theology within Protestantism, particularly in its liberal form; and
his influence is still forceful.

Schleiermacher's concern was to provide theology with academic credibility in the modern rationalistic university. He argued
that theology's task was essentially practical. Alongside doctors
and lawyers, the clergy were one of the ancient professions whose
training was traditionally the task of the university. One of the
characteristics of modern society has been the continual emergence of professional groups. But professional practice has to be
grounded in adequate theory. For the ministry and Church
organization, theology is precisely that theory. Theology is like a
tree. It has its roots in fundamental theology, including the history
and philosophy of religion, by which the credibility of faith is
established. The trunk, which gives the tree strength, is the systematic study of the tradition in Bible, history and doctrine. The
crown, bearing the fruit, is practical theology which looks at the
way the product of the theological enterprise is used in Church
and society. This, itself, is subdivided into numerous strands
which we have encountered before: variously, homiletics (preaching), liturgics (worship), catechetics (education), poimenics
(pastoral care), and diakonics (management and public service).

The strength of this model is that it takes authority seriously.
Christian action is indeed a response to God's call in Christ. We
live by grace and by gift and not in our own strength and desires.
There are given standards and norms. It is not surprising that
today, in a rapidly changing, fluid, pluralistic society in which
there seem to be no firm points of reference, many feel that there
is a need to hold on to some kind of external reference point. It
also takes academic theology seriously: the need to face the hard
questions of truth and wisdom in the world of intellectual
challenge.

The weaknesses of this model, however, are twofold. First it
suggests that theology is really the prerogative of the professional
structures of the Church. It therefore feeds the so-called 'clerical
paradigm'. But in our time there is, as we have seen in earlier
chapters, an awareness of the corporate nature of the people of
God. Theology is the heritage, voice and task of the whole
Church, not a specialist activity beyond the interest and reach of

others. Secondly, the process is unidirectional: from theory to practice. And this gives precedence to theory, making practice merely derivative. Real theology, it suggests, is located in the traditional academic interests of historical and philosophical enquiry.

We are finding out today, however, that there is no simple, deductive relationship between theory and practice. Rather there is a dialectical exchange between them. In theological terms: beliefs have been hammered out in the very practical struggles and controversies of Christian history; while at the same time the deeds of witness and service have been informed by a living faith. Take any of the great pivotal figures of Christianity – Athanasius, Augustine, Aquinas, Luther, Wesley, Barth – and their theology arises from and reflects back on to the challenges they had to face. It is this kind of realization that stimulates the renewed interest in the affinities between science and religion. For science too has ceased to see itself as detached theory and has begun to recognize that its own procedures are more complex and dialectical than once assumed. The model of applied theory is still, however, alive and well. It is the basis of much German practical theology as well as the working assumption of much traditional practical theology in Britain and elsewhere.

(i)   Schleiermacher, F., *Brief Outline on the Study of Theology* (John Knox 1966), is the classic text. The Barthian revelatory version of the model is well represented by Thurneysen, E., *A Theology of Pastoral Care* (John Knox 1962); Bonhoeffer, D., *Spiritual Care* (Fortress 1985); and Firet, J., *Dynamics in Pastoring* (Eerdmans 1986).

More recent Protestant pastoral theology has developed this tradition in dialogue with contemporary social science and theology; see: Heitink, G., *Practical Theology – History, Theory, Action Dynamics* (Eerdmans 1999).

For a critique of this approach see: Farley, Edward, *Theologia* (Fortress 1983).

(ii) For a Catholic model in the context of Vatican II see: Rahner, Karl, *Theology of Pastoral Action* (Burns and Oates 1968).

(iii) A similar approach from a British Methodist is found in Greeves, D., *Theology and the Cure of Souls* (Epworth 1960).

(iv) The conservative evangelical tradition with its emphasis on the primacy of Scripture takes a similar line. At its extreme, rejecting any help from modern human sciences, is Adams, J. More usually there is a serious creative engagement with sociological and psychological understandings within the framework of the theological perspective. See: Adams, Jay E., *More Than Redemption* (Baker Books 1979); Collins, G., *Christian Counselling* (Work 1980); Harding, R.F., *Roots and Shoots* (Hodder and Stoughton 1985), and *Pathways to Wholeness* (Hodder and Stoughton 1998); Atkinson, D.J. and Field, D.H., *New Dictionary of Christian Ethics and Pastoral Theology* (IVP 1995); Tidball, D., *Skilful Shepherds* (IVP 1997).

(v) There has been some interest in recovering and giving prominence to the wisdom of the tradition, led by Oden, T.C., *Pastoral Care in the Classic Tradition* (Fortress 1984); also: Purves, Andrew, *Pastoral Theology in the Classical Tradition* (Westminster/John Knox 2001); Evans, Gillian (ed.), *A History of Pastoral Care* (Cassell 2000).

The method of critical correlation

The modern renaissance of practical theology really got under way in the mid-1960s. The primary stimulus for this, as we saw in Chapter 1, was the rapid emergence of the social sciences and their related professions out of the Second World War. Education, social work, nursing and other groups developed new models of training that combined academic learning and field work, theoretical and critical models and induction into practice.[2] It was natural that theological education, especially for those training as clergy, should borrow from the new insights and skills that informed other caring professions. So practical theology increasingly became that part of the course where practical skills were taught for the professional clergy. This greatly enriched practical theology. But there was a risk: that the new humanistically based skills and insights could oust the theological grounding, or at least wag the tail of the theological dog. However much real gain was to be had, it sometimes appeared that the pastoral task was seldom different or distinctive from that of others in the caring field.

Not surprisingly there have been many voices raised against what looked like the total abdication of theological responsibility. How was it possible to recover the theological focus? Some, as has been noted above, tried to return to older models of practical theology in which the Bible or church teaching became the dominant element. Others, however, sought to retain the gains made from the human sciences while attempting to secure a theological recovery. It is this that lies behind the so-called method of critical correlation.

This approach has been most vigorously explored in North America, notably in Chicago under the stimulus of Don Browning. The departure point was the method of correlation of Paul Tillich.[3] Tillich suggested that the human questions concerning meaning and existence, which are flung by humanity at the universe, encounter a response from the gospel in the revelation given by God in Christ. So a dialogue is set up between question and answer; and answers should correlate with, respond to and challenge the question. Perhaps an apposite example is that of Martin Luther whose cry was, 'Where can I meet a loving God who can deal with my sense of sin?' The answer from reading Paul's Letter to the Romans was, paradoxically, that the righteousness of God is his love. We are justified by trust (faith). Out of that came the living truths that sustained the Reformation. There have been many variations on this theme. Here we can look briefly at three.

1. The first and most straightforward approach has been to talk about a dialogue with 'the tradition' or a theological perspective on the one hand, and the issue under consideration on the other. Thus the practical theologian stands on the frontier between the insights of Christian wisdom, based on Bible and tradition, and the reality of the present. James Whyte sees this as a threefold engagement between the theological disciplines, the social sciences and the actual situation.[4] A moment's thought, however, would make it clear that any situation is always highly complex, many-layered and on the move. Take an example like marrying a divorced person in church. Each person involved is working at many levels, relating to 'the tradition' and understanding the situation differently. As a result others, such as Michael Taylor or James Fowler, have offered more complex models to account for the richness of reality. But in the end the model threatens to be as confusing as the actual situation. It is perhaps better to work with a simple model that is a framework for reflection while recognizing that, in the concrete situation, there are subtleties that have to be served in a creative and open way. There is, however, one obvious advantage to this model. Unlike the earlier ones, this

approach is not predisposed to keep practical theology as a discipline primarily for the professional group. The correlational method can be used over the whole of Christian concern. Indeed some of the most obvious examples of this way of working have been the reports on public issues drawn up by different church Boards of Social Responsibility. Whatever their merits or demerits the attempt has been to set alongside each other the imperatives of the gospel and of the social realities.

2. The second expression of the correlation method brings together pastoral concerns and ethics. In working with individuals and groups, pastoral care is concerned to facilitate personal or corporate growth. Very often, if not inevitably, some kind of ethical dimension is involved. So, for example, when a couple come to a minister to request a wedding some time will be given to helping them look again at the commitments they are undertaking. This will include ensuring they are being realistic about different aspects of family life and, if necessary, suggesting points at which further consideration may be appropriate. Interpersonal relations of that kind are of the very essence of ethics. Rarely are ethical decisions obvious, clear-cut choices. Rather they are about how we value people, the norms and expectations we have of each other, what society expects, and what we look for. Ethical behaviour depends on the quality of people: are they trustworthy, kind, open; or are they devious, angry, selfish? The task of practical theology is to become aware of how different levels of personality and experience impinge on the particular situation; and to ask how we can better understand it in order to enable people to make more Christian decisions. To do this, we need to know something about the social and personal context, how people tick and what is going on. It has been Don Browning who has most insistently worked on this theme. He offers a fivefold pattern, a kind of checklist of different factors that affect each and every situation. We act out of many levels: memory, culture, social pressures, faith, personal history, as well as choice and desire. The pastor helps people or groups to become aware of and relate to each of these. The problem is that, on occasion, Browning appears to subsume practical theology under ethics; that is, the ethical provides both the parameters and the methodology of practical theology. This would appear to be too strongly stated. They are indeed closely associated but pastoral care is not to be equated with ethical demand. Rather the primary concern is to discover

grace. What is the gift of God in this situation? Grace may and
does demand response but is not defined by it. If anything, ethics
is a sub-set of practical theology. Ethics specifically asks 'What
must I do?', but within the wider setting of 'Where am I?' and
'Who am I?' This is the burden of so many of Jesus' parables. First
there is the realization of my place in the presence of a gracious
God. That releases my choice and response. In the prodigal son
story the point is precisely that the father makes no demands on
either son, however much he may have wished for them. We are
not even given the next step in the story. The great strength of
Browning's position, which he shares with David Tracy, is that
practical theology must be a public activity. The virtue of ethical
reasoning is that it attempts to persuade people in the market
place of ideas and action. There is a rational and open argument
that is accessible to anyone and with which anyone can disagree.
To revert to the example of a particular report on public issues,
Faith in the City[5] was clearly a public document. It was not only
addressed to both Church and nation, it also argued its case on
the basis of evidence and rational debate in the light of a belief
that was openly defended.

3. The third of the correlation models bases itself on the widespread interest in hermeneutics. Hermeneutics is the study of the
processes of interpretation. Its concern is how humans communicate, and how meaning, intention, and truth, are conveyed and
shared. The basic example is the interpretation of a text. The document is a human product by which one person communicates to
another. Within theology this has obvious direct application to the
Bible. But, as we all know, the interpretation of the Bible is not
straightforward. There are problems of translation, historical and
cultural distance and so forth. But equally there has to be an
awareness of how we come to the text, how it is used, what we are
looking for and what authority it is given. The Bible is read and
interpreted in a complex, diverse and moving dynamic context.
This is what makes it so elusive and yet so exciting. It is like
coming back time and again to a favourite place which is changing with the light of day, the weather, the seasons and the years. It
is always the same yet always different, familiar yet ever new. What
is true of the Bible and of written texts is surely only a particular
instance of all human social existence. Pastoral relationships, for
example, are the interaction of people who seek to understand
each other and need to 'read' who they each are. Our lives are

living human documents. And we have to reach out to each other, see, hear, feel and comprehend how the other is. Although in a pastoral context there may be much in common between those talking to each other, there are always differences. The circles of my experience cannot coincide with the circles of your experience, however much they overlap. This discrepancy will be even greater between strangers for whom the present encounter may be the only point of contact. To use hermeneutical language, these 'horizons' have to be merged through a process of understanding and empathy so that there can be a meaningful dialogue. The hermeneutical model can, therefore, provide a framework for understanding this process. It asks what is happening to both (or more) parties at the different levels of dialogue: cultural, historical, social, psychological, metaphysical, ethical and so forth. How do we live together with shared meanings and yet in diversity and responsibility? Perhaps a good example is John Hull's autobiographical diary *On Sight and Insight*.[6] He brilliantly conveys what it is like to go blind and to rediscover his world in darkness. It is his own hermeneutical journey, interpreting himself to himself; but it is also his interpretation of himself to us so that we can enter into his world. Yet it is not our world (even if we too are blind); though our lives, having met him, are never the same again. His horizon, to some extent, has been drawn into ours and ours into his. There is shared experience and meaning.

Hermeneutics alerts us to another dimension of the human condition that has been taken up into pastoral practice, both personal and social. We live out of our own story. When we are asked who we are, the most natural response is to begin to flesh out our history: where we were born, our education, the work we do, the people and incidents that have formed us. Two points are being made. Personal and community truth is to be found primarily in story and not in propositions. We come out of a past and live by a tradition – a tradition that is both highly personal (this is me, unique) and part of a wider story that includes neighbourhoods, class, culture, religion, ethnicity and nationality. This leads to the second point. Story is how we relate to others. In a conversation at a party we not only tell about ourselves but search for common ground with others: shared interests, shared acquaintances, shared places. We tell each other stories, anecdotes and happenings. We find that our story overlaps with others, which gives us a bonding. Even when arguing a point, whether for an ethical choice or a political choice, an aesthetic preference or metaphysical belief, the discussion inevitably includes narrative elements, whether personal or historical, presented as a form of logic. This is the nature of time-bound beings.

Theologically the Church is the fellowship of a common story. At its heart is the story of Jesus, crucified and risen, that gives shape and meaning to the Christian story. The call to faith is to find our story, in its uniqueness and yet part of a wider whole, bound up in and moulded by the story of Jesus. The 'old, old story' is not merely a rehearsal of past events, though that is crucial, but a present story that accompanies us. Through it we find that our story is not 'a tale told by an idiot . . . signifying nothing' (*Macbeth* 5.7.62) but is part of the cosmic story at the heart of the universe. At the same time this means that we dwell in at least two stories – that of the gospel and those of our own time and place. Often these clash, as when Christian commitment runs counter to our cultural setting. While we 'cannot serve two masters' (Matt. 6.24) it is impossible to escape the tension. We have to work out how to weave these together in faith.

No wonder, then, that narrative theology has been of such interest to practical theology and pastoral ministry. The Bible itself is largely story. It tells the story of creation and salvation in the stories of Israel, Jesus and the early Church. It is little wonder that one of the contemporary emphases in trying to make the Bible come alive in a generation that has lost its roots in the Christian story is to try to re-encounter that story through different media, following the age-old tradition of Christian art, drama and oratory. This is also taken up in pastoral care, worship and personal meditation by entering into the drama of Scripture or in recognizing the spiritual reality in the story of others. Indeed, it is argued that doctrines, which seem to be freestanding statements, are in fact distillations of and reflections on the experience of the Christian community as it has encountered God through faith, thought and action. This draws us into the centrality and nature of theological reflection (see Chapter 9).

(i) SPCK's Library of Pastoral Care has been of proven worth, usually addressing a single issue, but some of its volumes have been criticized for exhibiting a tendency to dissolve theology into therapy. Also, for example, Clinebell, H., *Basic Types of Pastoral Care and Counselling* (SCM 1984).

(ii) The demand for a reappraisal is usefully surveyed and given a response in Pattison, S., *A Critique of Pastoral Care* (SCM 2000). Two classical expressions of the reintroduction of theology into practical theology: Lambourne, R.A., *Community, Church and Healing* (Darton, Longman and Todd 1963); Campbell, A., *Rediscovering Pastoral Care* (Darton, Longman and Todd 1981).

(iii) The manifesto of the 'critical correlation method' was Browning, D. (ed.), *Practical Theology – the Emerging Field in Theology* (Harper and Row 1983); see also Mudge, Lewis S. and Poling, James, *Formation and Reflection* (Fortress 1987); examples of the model: Taylor, Michael, H., *Learning to Care* (SPCK 1983); and Whitehead, J. and E., *Method in Ministry* (Seabury 1981); Lyall, David, *The Integrity of Pastoral Care* (SPCK 2001) is a good working example.

(iv) The ethical model is expounded in Browning, Don, *The Moral Context of Pastoral Care* (Westminster 1976); *Religious Ethics and Pastoral Care* (Fortress 1983); Noyce, Gaylord, *The Minister as Moral Counsellor* (Fortress 1989); Atkinson, D., *Pastoral Ethics* (Lynx 1994).

(v) The 'hermeneutical model' in theology is set out in Tracy, David, *The Analogical Imagination* (SCM 1981); Louth, Andrew, *Discerning the Mystery* (Clarendon 1983); Thiselton, Anthony, *New Horizons in Hermeneutics* (HarperCollins 1992); Green, Garrett, *Theology, Hermeneutics and Imagination* (CUP 1999); Stiver, Dan R., *Theology after Ricoeur* (Westminster/John Knox 2001); Bartholomew, C. *et al.* (eds), *After Pentecost: Language and Biblical Interpretation* (Paternoster 2001); Briggs, Richard, *Words in Action: Speech and Act Theory and Biblical Interpretation* (T&T Clark 2001); Bradt, Kevin, *Story as a Way of Knowing* (Sheed and Ward 1997). On doctrine and narrative: Lindbeck, George A. *The Nature of Doctrine: Religion and Theology in a Postliberal Age* (SPCK 1984). In pastoral practice, including story: Capps, Donald, *Pastoral Care and Hermeneutics* (Fortress 1984); Gerkin, C.V., *The Living Human Document* (Abingdon 1984); *Prophetic Pastoral Practice* (Abingdon 1991); *An Introduction to Pastoral Care* (Abingdon 1997); Capps, D., *Reframing: A New Method in Pastoral Care* (Fortress 1990); Simpkinson C. and A. (eds), *Sacred Stories: A Celebration of the Power of Stories to Transform and Heal* (HarperCollins

1993); Wimberly, E.P., *Using Scripture in Pastoral Counselling* (Abingdon 1994); Anderson, H. and Foley, E., *Mighty Stories; Dangerous Rituals – Weaving Together the Human and the Divine* (Jossey Bass 1998); Neuger, C.C., *Counselling Women: a Narrative Pastoral Approach* (Fortress 2001); Mudge, Lewis, *Rethinking the Beloved Community – Ecclesiology, Hermeneutics and Social Theory* (WCC 2001); Quicke, Michael J., *360 Degrees Preaching: Hearing, Seeing and Living the Word* (Baker 2003); Ballard, Paul and Holmes, Stephen R., *The Bible in Pastoral Practice* (Darton, Longman and Todd 2005).

(vi) Cross-cultural practice, especially in a pluralistic society, is increasingly important. See, e.g. Augsburger, D.W., *Pastoral Counselling Across Cultures* (John Knox 1986); Lartey, Emmanuel Y., *In Living Colour – An Intercultural Approach to Pastoral Care and Counselling* (Cassell 1997). For a more theoretical and theological discussion see: Shorter, Aylward, *Toward a Theology of Inculturation* (Chapman 1988); Bosch, David, *Transforming Mission* (Orbis 1991).

Praxis models for practical theology

The third group of models for practical theology starts at a different place. The concept of praxis comes out of the Marxist tradition. It is an attempt to overcome the rationalistic distinction between theory and practice which we noted in the first model.

The starting point is the present, concrete situation; that is, current praxis. But praxis is more than practice, for it recognizes that no human activity is value-free. What is happening today is an expression of human assumptions about how things must or ought to happen. Thus I go to work in the morning because I am caught up in that pattern of social reality. I may sometimes wonder why, but I almost certainly acquiesce. However, if I am really to get a grip of my situation, it has to be analysed in depth. That is, to use a well-known phrase of Habermas, I have to have a 'hermeneutic (interpretive tool) of suspicion'. It is necessary to ask, what is really going on? Who controls? Who gains? Who loses? Who suffers? Thus when I go to work I can begin to realize that maybe I am after all only a cipher in someone else's machine. It is not all really for my benefit. In Marxist analysis, of course, it is always assumed that the economic power structures are basic. But that is only one level of truth. The same principle can be applied to, for example, cultural pressure or assumptions about values and worth.

The first task, then, is to subject everything to an analytical critique, including the perspective of the analyst. Then, in Christian reflection, comes the need to recover the basic gospel imperative. This provides the attitude which should inform the critical praxis that follows the analysis. This is to be found in the biblical perspective on the situation: the option for the poor and the struggle for liberation. Out of the juxtaposition of analysis and gospel emerges the new praxis, which itself has to be subject to the same process.

Perhaps the best known of all examples of this methodology comes from the base communities of Latin America. The Bible and the sacraments become both the inspiration for and the means of a critical understanding of the situation. Poverty is seen as injustice and discipleship is found in the struggle for change. This is the practical heart of liberation theology.

The basic approach, however, has been taken up much more widely, well beyond the bounds of those who would call themselves liberationists. So, for example, there are expressions of radical discipleship among conservative evangelicals and also within the more mainstream denominations. There are also other radical theologies seeking to work from the experience of the marginalized, such as feminist theology, black theology and Third World theologies such as Minjong Theology from Korea. It can also be seen that there are points of convergence with the 'critical correlation' models outlined above. So a growing consensus begins to emerge.

This consensus is most frequently symbolized by the widespread use of the so-called 'pastoral cycle' (see Chapter 6). There are numerous variations and refinements of this basic method but despite the risk of over-simplification, the most usual is a fourfold cycle. This approach starts with the present situation, which is subject to analysis to reveal the truth of what is going on. Then comes the stage of theological reflection, asking how the gospel should be heard in these circumstances, elucidating the path of Christian obedience. On this basis plans can be laid, targets set out, resources deployed. In its turn this leads to action which becomes the basis for further reflection. This is the model that will shape the second part of this book as we consider various aspects of doing practical theology.

The strength of this approach is that it is anchored in the practical. Theological activity, including the more theoretical study of the Bible and doctrine, serves this practical end. This is exemplified in the status given to the theologian in a liberation theology context. There is no denial of the value of the historical or dogmatic theologian, but theology's task in the end is to be a resource at the disposal of the people of God in their quest for obedience.

Moreover, it takes seriously the experience of the Church in its struggle. It is lived faith which is an important and primary source of theological understanding. Theology has to listen to how people experience their belief. This is why the sociological and psychological study of faith in practice is so important. Out of the actual ways faith and practice impinge on each other come new insights. For example, if women articulate their sense of oppression in a male-dominated Church and society and find Christianity becomes real in ways not previously understood, then the Church has to take due note, and theological perspectives and language may have to change.

Of course there are dangers and shortcomings. Like all models it can be over-simplistic and induce short cuts. There can be a tendency to activism and a playing down of reflection and personal spirituality. There can also be a theological fundamentalism that replaces one fixed dogmatic structure with another and is impatient with the need to develop a sensitive and creative approach to theological reflection. Liberation praxis has to be equally as much subjected to analysis as the praxis it sets out to criticize and change.

(i)   For an introduction to liberation theology: Cadorette, C. *et al.* (eds), *Liberation Theology – An Introductory Reader* (Orbis 1992). For a wider view of political theologies: Bevans, S.B., *Models of Contextual Theology* (Orbis 1992); also Schreiter, R.J., *Constructing Local Theologies* (SCM 1985).

(ii) For a general introduction to praxis as a philosophical issue: Lobkowicz, Nicholas, *Theory and Practice – from Aristotle to Marx* (Notre Dame 1967); Morris, Peter, *Meaning and Action* (Routledge and Kegan Paul 1987).

(iii) Examples of praxis style theology and practice: Amirtham, S. and Pobee, J.S., *Theology by the People* (WCC 1986); Fraser, I.M., *Reinventing Theology as the People's Task* (Wild Goose 1988); Green, L., *Let's Do Theology* (Mowbray

1990); Poling, James, *The Abuse of Power* (Abingdon 1991); Pattison, Stephen, *Pastoral Care and Liberation Theology* (CUP 1994).

(iv) From the radical evangelical end: Sheppard, David, *Bias to the Poor* (Hodder and Stoughton 1983); Wallis, Jim, *The Call to Conversion* (Lion 1982); Yoder, John, *The Original Revolution* (Herald 1971); Sugden, Christopher, *Radical Discipleship* (Marshalls 1981).

(v) For a sympathetic introduction to black theology: Witvliet, Theo, *The Way of the Black Messiah* (SCM 1987); Wimberley, Edward, *Claiming God, Reclaiming Dignity – African–American Pastoral Care* (Abingdon 2003).

(vi) Gender issues. Feminism has been the most prominent. Introductions to feminist theology: Loades, Ann, *Feminist Theology – A Reader* (SPCK 1993); Soskice, Janet Martin and Lipton, Diane, *Feminist Theology* (OUP 2003). More recently male agendas have caught the attention: Pryce, Mark, *Finding a Voice – Men, Women and the Community of the Church* (SCM 1996); Neuger, C.C. and Poling, James N., *The Care of Men* (Abingdon 1997). For gay concerns: Heskins, Jeffrey, *Unheard Voices* (Darton, Longman and Todd 2001).

(vii) Modern Marxian thought and critical theory are making greater impact on practical theology: Graham, Elaine, *Transforming Practice* (Mowbray 1996); Schuld, J. Joyce, *Foucault and Augustine – Reconsidering Power and Law* (Notre Dame 2003); also promised *Michel Foucault, an Introduction for Theologians* (CUP).

The habitus model

There is, however, a fourth model which can be designated the habitus model, a phrase which is borrowed from Edward Farley.[7] 'Habitus' has the basic meaning of the more usual word 'habit'. But for us, habit is something which we do without thinking; it is almost beyond our control. In classical ethical thought, however, a habit is a mind-set that has become second nature, but which has been induced by long training. Of course there can be bad habits and good habits. A good habit is a virtue (courage, love, etc.) which is so ingrained that it has got beyond deliberate ethical choice. We act well because that disposition is there, part of the soul. It is very like the way the military are so trained that they know automatically how to react under fire.

So the task of theology, and practical theology in particular, is not in the end to provide methodology or skills, but a training of mind and heart. On this account the aim is to build up the body of Christ in every way. It may be necessary to engage in processes of enquiry, analysis and decision-making, but at the point where it matters in daily living in society what is needed is a Christian instinct and a Christian nerve. This is far from abdicating the demands of discipline. It is a long and continuous task, demanding care and commitment. It engages every part of the personality – not least the intellect. It is constantly fed by learning and discovery about the world and about the faith. But it also insists on keeping together mind and heart, for it is also about the will and emotions. In other words we are concerned with building spirituality: 'The fear of the Lord is the beginning of wisdom' (Prov. 1.7). In the New Testament, to be wise is to have the mind of Christ, to live on the wavelength of the Spirit. It is to share in the joy and sorrow, in the creativity and sacrifice of God himself.

This is not a new thought. Indeed it is perhaps foundational to theology. The Eastern tradition in many ways reflects the thought of the early, patristic, classical era of Christian history. Theology did not start off as a systematic intellectual pursuit or as a distinctive activity done by special persons. That was a medieval development, when theology became a science. The earlier understanding is that theology is literally 'God-talk' or better 'God-wisdom' and was therefore mediated in a myriad of ways; in liturgy and prayer, in sermon and teaching, in discussion and writing. Orthodoxy does not simply mean 'right belief' but 'right glory': that is, knowing, speaking of and worshipping God aright in sacrament and in life.

It is a tradition that has continued to be present in some form or other. Thomas Aquinas understood the end of theology to be the vision of God. In the pietistic and conservative evangelical traditions formal theology has always been understood as formative of the Christian character. Karl Barth called theology an act of praise in response to the goodness of God in Christ, the disciple's response in understanding. Urs von Balthasar found the way to God in the contemplation of beauty.

Such a disposition of the heart cannot be taught, but it may begin to grow because there are occasions and opportunities to learn, reflect, contemplate and pray. It is a part of our personal journey, of being open to the Spirit. It is good, therefore, to remember that practical theology is not only about the demands of discipleship and the task of the Church in the world. It is not only about the needs of persons and communities. It is also about oneself, of growing into Christ and of living in the fellowship of saints. It is also about losing oneself in God.

Thus ministerial training is essentially about developing the Christian character. This will involve a realistic self-awareness of strengths and weaknesses, of gifts and limitations to be offered in pastoral service. It will mean developing habits of prayer and devotion which enable the centre of one's being to hold firm in God. It means discovering the path of pilgrimage and growth. It is this that has been at the heart of the English tradition in pastoral training, both Anglican and Nonconformist. The theological college developed out of the apprenticeship model, whereby trainees were attached to experienced and wise practioners who passed on the habits of wisdom as much as practical skills. It is this that is being sought under the rubric and practice of 'theological reflection'.

The same goes for the aim of pastoral practice. It is to enable the whole Christian community, personally and collectively, to grow in grace and Christian wisdom; to provide a resource that will stand one in good stead in the hurly-burly of life. It may sound old fashioned, but the task is to produce Christian men and women who in their daily situation live out their faith without fuss. The wonder of it is that there are so many who, unwittingly, through the normal routines of faith, have become the salt of the earth and lights in dark places.

Alongside this has been the emerging focus on 'virtue ethics' as an approach to pastoral practice. In this perspective ethical norms and practice are not to be derived from some kind of normative rational or revealed principles but arise from the life of the community or culture. The members of that grouping indwell the moral world into which they have been socialized. In a pluralistic society there may be competing cultural patterns, of which one may be the Church. To be a Christian is to be a disciple (a learner) who by participation in the life, ritual and educative processes of the community of faith is drawn into its ethical understanding and practice. Thus the aim is so to indwell the social reality that it becomes a 'habitus'. There have been numerous critiques of such an understanding, ranging from the possibility of oppressive conformity to the question of how to judge one's own or others' standards. But this is, in fact, how we are socialized and, in this context, underlines the importance of the tradition.

(i)   The habitus model is set out in Farley, E., *Theologia* (Fortress 1983); see also: Holmes, U.T., *Ministry and Imagination* (Seabury 1976); Tomlinson, Anne L., *Training God's Spies – Developing the Imagination in Theological Formation* (Contact Pastoral Trust 2001).

(ii) The modern writer who has constantly looked at the relation between ministry and spirituality has been Nouwen, Henri: *Creative Ministry* (Doubleday 1971); *The Wounded Healer* (Doubleday 1972); *Reaching Out* (Collins 1975). See also: Ecclestone, Alan, *Yes to God* (Darton, Longman and Todd 1975); Holmes, U.T., *Spirituality for Ministry* (Morehouse 1982); Leech, Kenneth, *Spirituality and Pastoral Care* (Sheldon 1986); a Catholic resource in Wicks, Robert J. (ed.), *A Handbook of Spirituality for ministers* (2 vols) (Paulist 1995 and 2000).

(iii) The debate about virtue ethics was introduced by MacIntyre, Alasdair, *After Virtue – A Study in Moral Theory* (Duckworth 1985). See also Hauerwas, Stanley, *The Peaceable Kingdom* (SCM 1984); Colwell, John, *Living the Christian Story* (T&T Clark 2001). Pastorally: Hauerwas, Stanley and Williman, W.R., *Resident Aliens* (Abingdon 1989); Clark, Neville, *Pastoral Care in Context* (Mayhew 1992); Goodliff, Paul, *Care in a Confused Climate* (Darton, Longman and Todd 1998).

Notes

1   'The Enlightenment' is a title given in the history of thought to the dominant intellectual tendency in Western culture. It was largely oriented by four fundamental characteristics: (i) a commitment to reason as the proper tool and final authority for determining issues; (ii) the appeal to what is natural; (iii) an idea of progress; (iv) rejection of the authority of tradition. Pailin, David A. in Richardson, A. and Bowden, J., *A New Dictionary of Christian Theology* (SCM 1983).

2   See Chapter 1.

3   See McKelway, Alexander J., *The Systematic Theology of Paul Tillich* (Lutterworth 1964), pp. 45–8.

4 In Campbell, Alastair, *A Dictionary of Pastoral Care* (SPCK 1987).
5 Church House Publishing 1985.
6 Hull, John, *On Sight and Insight* (One World 1997).
7 Farley, Edward, *Theologia* (Fortress 1983), pp. 35–6.

PART II
The Art of Practical Theology

Chapter 6

Tools for practical theology – introducing the pastoral cycle

The first part of this book set practical theology into its broad context. Two sets of questions were posed. The first asked what kind of activity practical theology is. How does it relate to other theological disciplines? Who does practical theology? Is there room for a specialist activity? The general conclusion was that there is indeed a recognizable formal theological discipline called practical theology. It is however, on the one hand, one of a cluster of disciplines each of which contributes to the whole theological enterprise and, on the other hand, a particular way of doing theology that should inform and influence all theology as an essentially practical activity.

The second set of questions looked at in Part I attempted to tease out a major theoretical issue that shapes how practical theology is carried out. That issue was the relationship between theory and practice which underlies the several models and approaches to practical theology which are in current use. The discussion suggested that there is indeed considerable diversity which in a growing discipline needs to be resolved: but at the same time, there is considerable common ground in the actual doing of practical theology.

Part II starts from that point. The primary aim is to look at some specific issues raised by the doing of practical theology. This will include such things as: working from experience; drawing on the social sciences and relating them to theology; what is meant by theological reflection; and how action and spirituality inform each other. There is no intention of setting out a specific, detailed syllabus. The content and methods of practical theology are always related to the actual task in hand, the resources available and the particular context. But practical theology is properly thought of as having certain trade marks such as experiential learning, starting from as well as addressing the practice of ministry, and serving both the Church and the world. So in Part II we are offering a number of guiding principles and skills, insights and pointers which can be a resource to teachers, students and practitioners in the field.

First, however, it is necessary to address a prior issue. Is it possible to offer a focal core for this process which can begin to draw together into some coherence the diversity of concern and approach that is inherent in practical theology? The suggestion, as we have already indicated in the last chapter, is that the pastoral cycle provides a methodological tool that does indeed take account of the strengths and weaknesses of the various models listed above, and also provides some kind of structure for thinking about practical theology which allows both flexibility and diversity.

Describing the pastoral cycle

The pastoral cycle has become widely used in practical theology, and there are a number of variations on the theme. While its popularity has been comparatively recent, it is possible to discern similar approaches from an earlier period. An example would be the 'see–judge–act' model of Fr Joseph Cadijn's Catholic Action between the wars.[1] In contemporary practical theology, however, the pastoral cycle owes its origin to the extensive and pervasive influence of liberation theology since the 1960s. In Latin America the 'base Christian communities' have developed this approach as a means to structure their theological and social critique and action. It is now in common usage, even in circles that would not consider themselves influenced by liberationist tendencies. Others would claim to have developed the method independently. In different forms it can be found, for example, in radical evangelical circles, in industrial mission, in urban mission and community development.[2] This action–reflection model of learning is now also prominent in the training of teachers, social workers, nurses and other professionals. Emphasis is placed on the substantial experience on placement in the work setting which is then used as material for reflection and learning in the more formal educational environment. It is now also becoming commonplace in professional or practical theological education. Some whole schemes are built round it. As we have noted previously, there seems to be a growing convergence.

Such widespread acceptance clearly suggests that the pastoral cycle should be at the heart of any contemporary perspective on practical theology. The proposal here, however, is that the cycle is not just a useful tool but can provide a focus that draws together the different emphases found in the discipline into a coherent and yet flexible whole. It can do this in part because it is already rooted in a theological practice. Thus the subsequent chapters take up the phases of the cycle. It is also argued in the later part of this chapter that the pastoral cycle can respond to the theological concerns exhibited in each of the approaches to practical theology described in the last chapter. The result is that they may be seen to complement each other rather than be regarded as alternatives. Each emphasizes a particular theological need but each needs the others to make a theological whole.

But first it is necessary to set out what the pastoral cycle is.

Sheila is the Free Church minister to a group of village congregations. As she settled into the new experience it became increasingly clear that all was not well in the community. Outwardly things appeared normal and even prosperous. The seasonal round had its traditional highlights – the village fête, the show, harvest supper, cricket on the green. Community groups, Young Farmers, British Legion, WI, the football club, church and chapel were busy. Yet there were long-term changes afoot which Sheila could see had already eroded the rural community and would bring further changes. Neither the churches nor anyone else seemed to be aware of the threat, or to care much. She found a few who shared her concern but there was little that could be done. People did not want their idyllic notion of 'the village' shattered.

Then all hell broke loose. The County Education Committee wanted to close down the Junior School in one of the villages. The anger, anxiety and panic were extraordinary. To lose the school was more than an issue about education and child safety. The schools were at the centre of village life, giving meeting space to organizations and providing playing fields for the whole community. No longer would a teacher live and work in the village. Sheila was promptly caught up in all the protest: organizing committees, running petitions, arguing the case here, there and everywhere. The interesting thing was that the campaign group was an odd alliance of mums that lived in the small council estate on the edge of the village and the new, immigrant, middle-class younger families whose children enjoyed the intimate atmosphere of a small school.

But there was a more profound effect because the threat to the school tore off the façade and made the community face itself. Suddenly it was clear that the village was more of a commuter suburb than an agricultural centre. Farming was going through a crisis. There was a hidden poverty, not least among the apparently affluent. And the community was fragmented and bewildered. Divisions became apparent between the older farming community, the incomers, and the agricultural 'industrial' workers.

For Sheila there were three outcomes. First was the recognition of real poverty, especially on the council estate: low wages, high unemployment, single parent families. The erosion of the village – closed shops, run down public transport and so on – hit harder than she imagined. It was through the campaign group that it was possible to get alongside some of the families. Slowly, not least because of the help of Jean the community nurse, it was possible to gather a group together and to work at ways of countering the downward spiral. So a playgroup was formed, using the chapel hall at no charge; co-operative use of such things as power tools was arranged; by giving grants the Council encouraged a scheme for self-help community maintenance on the council houses and in public buildings, supervised by local skilled labour; help was given in finding jobs or looking at career changes through the Citizens' Advice Bureau.

Secondly, Sheila found it easier to talk with her friends about the deeper problems of rural life and changing social patterns. Another group was formed, unofficial yet fairly representative of the different interests: the doctor, a teacher, a social worker, the vicar and local farmers, leading figures in the community, young people and some of the parents from the estate. Here was an instrument for reconciliation and hope, as they began to identify common tasks and to stimulate community action.

Thirdly, it was also possible to discern and encourage change in the congregation. Some members were directly involved in the school debate and the community action. But none were unaffected by the general upheaval. It was possible to draw other church members in to help with different projects or to meet special needs as they arose. One or two were part of the new community study group. Most importantly, however, a subtle shift was found in worship. Prayer became more relevant and Bible study felt more realistic. The small prayer group discovered the pain and joy of linking prayer and life. The Bible spoke directly about the poor or how to discern the Spirit in times of crisis. But Sunday worship, too, with its greater formality, took on an edge of purpose and expectation. And there was a recognition that the Chapel too (whose membership was mainly rooted in the past, although it had gained one or two new families) was itself both part of the problem and yet could be an instrument for change, if it was prepared for change itself.

A year later, after the immediate crisis had quietened down, Sheila was able to look back, and she found that something else stood out for her. Yes, there were signs of a new mood in the village and the several initiatives continued. But what struck her also was how much she, and with her the Christian community, had learnt and changed. There was a wider and deeper vision of mission and ministry. She had now really become part of the community, accepted and recognized. Christian faith, she had discovered, involved being the servant of God in the service of the community (2 Cor. 4.5).

She had also made another discovery. A book given as a Christmas present had introduced her to a thing called the pastoral cycle. But she had in fact already been treading a similar path.

Sheila's story is unique to her. Yet it is not so uncommon. The pastoral cycle provides a formal outline analysis of a process such as has been described; it enables us to see more clearly and thus, if necessary, to help the process along. Perhaps, if she had known about it, it could have proved a useful vehicle for conscious reflection on what had been happening and saved a few mistakes. It was good, however, to feel that what books suggested in formal descriptions actually corresponded to experience. Normally the cycle is described as a fourfold action:

(i) **Experience**. The starting point is the present situation; the more-or-less routine existence of a given context. But there is a further element. This present is interrupted, whether from within or – as in Sheila's case – from outside by events that demand a response, or uncover a tension. It is no longer possible to go on as before.

(ii) **Exploration**. Any considered response must be based on an analysis of what is going on. This demands information and discussion. Much of that will come out of the experience of those involved. But, for example, to make a case to the Education Committee, the evidence cannot be anecdotal but must be systematic, digested and tested. It may be that more information has to be gathered from outside sources, or advice taken from experts.

(iii) **Reflection**. Information, by itself, does not give answers; it only indicates possibilities. There are other matters that have to be taken into consideration: personal and communal beliefs about how the world works, the purpose of life, moral values as to what is important and worth pursuing. It was in the light of her faith that Sheila allowed herself to be involved in the affairs of the village. But she also found herself working alongside others with whom she shared common ground on what was significant and valuable about people and community. Reflection, however, also includes discovery and change. It is part of being willing to recognize that all is not well; of acknowledging how things really are and not how we suppose them or wish them to be. In the village it was necessary for people to recognize that it was not a bucolic haven or a changeless Eden but a village exposed to the harsh realities of agricultural business economics and technological change, and disadvantaged in the economies of scale. Only then is it possible to take up a different, more realistic and creative stance. Perceptions, beliefs and values face the challenge of being in touch with contemporary realities.

(iv) **Action**. This comes out of the whole process on the basis of informed decisions and appropriate initiatives. Thus the school campaign group was able to mount an effective counter to the Education Committee's decision; or the Chapel could decide on new uses for its premises or how to express its new vision in the community.

The cycle, however, does not stop. There is now a new starting point. Sheila, looking back, recognizes that both she and the situation have changed. So the next stage must take that into account. Perhaps it is time now, by way of example, to look at the organization of the fête and to make it more comprehensive of the whole village? So the pastoral cycle is really a spiral, moving on all the time.

When looked at like this the pastoral cycle appears to be a straightforward description of a normal, everyday process. So, why bother to describe it? To have such a model, however, serves a very useful purpose. Most of the time life goes on without the need to worry about its mechanisms. But from time to time it is useful to have a check-list on the processes being used. It is all too easy to forget the obvious, to take short cuts or to jump a stage. That is why, especially in organizations, it is useful to review the situation and to reconsider the aims and objectives. Moreover, having a model makes it easier to initiate the process deliberately. Sheila's study group could be thought of as providing an audit for the whole community, consciously going through the cycle. In her congregation, proposals for action are put formally to a meeting where the cycle provides an outline for the formal processing of the suggestions. A widely used and valuable expression of this methodology is the Parish or Mission Audit (see Chapter 7).

Having said that, however, a warning must be issued. A model is a very limited tool. It is necessarily a simplified analysis of a process which is inevitably subtle and complex and rough at the edges. Nor does it work automatically. It is a guide and not a chain. Slavish adherence to a model can inhibit freedom and creativity. The cycle may not even proceed in a regular order. There may be a number of cycles interwoven together. Nevertheless, as a way of learning to appreciate the processes of human action it can prove invaluable.

The pastoral cycle as a theological tool

The pastoral cycle is a heuristic tool; that is, it provides a means of understanding and using a process of discovery and action. But as the focus of practical theology it must also provide a means of handling and relating theological activity. This is, then, the second task for this chapter: to find ways of drawing together the four approaches to practical theology in such a way as to affirm them positively while modifying them in the light of critical reflection. This is going to be done by suggesting a number of basic principles which inform practical theology and which relate to different aspects of the pastoral cycle.

Practical theology comes out of shared experience

The pastoral cycle, it has been noted, comes out of the experience of the basic Christian communities. It represents a methodology that reflects an underlying discovery: that practical truth arises from a common process of discovery which involves equally all who share in it. It was Paulo Freire who contrasted two educational models.[3] The dominant Western model is hierarchical and authoritarian. It invests the power of knowledge and skills in the expert who teaches or acts on behalf of the taught. The liberationist model gives authority and power to the taught as well as to the teacher because each has a contribution to make and each learns from the other in a shared enterprise. Thus, especially in the Christian context where the aim is precisely to enlarge a person's freedom and ability, it is important that everyone is seen to be contributing and thus of value.

Dominique Barbé[4] describes a meeting at which everyone is invited to tell what has happened to them since they last met:

> Very often at the beginning we hear something like this: 'Who me? Nothing interesting. As usual . . .' She has let the word slip: nothing interesting. But even the most ordinary story is of interest, for it has the texture of the sacred story. In it the Christian can see the narrative of each person's sacred story. So the peasant woman in her burden of poverty is as important to the group as the priest with all his training or the doctor with all her skills.

Barbé goes on to show how this interpretation of story allows the tellers to link into the biblical narrative and thus to be seen to be incorporated into the drama of salvation. It allows those who live in oppressive situations to find themselves in characters of the Bible who live the same reality, and thereupon to see how grace operates its salvation in them and in us – a true liberation of the whole being, individual and social.

And out of that growing solidarity and recognition of a new possibility comes what he calls 'the exodus of action'. For the group Barbé was actually referring to the action was to build a hut for a pregnant widow with ten children in defiance of officialdom. For Sheila and those round her it was to recognize that all in the village, old and new, poor and affluent, skilled and disadvantaged, belonged to a common history, whose lives are woven together.

They were all responsible for each other and could receive from each other. Thus whatever counsels or actions that have to be taken, they have to be as far as possible owned together and for mutual benefit. It was a hard lesson to learn but in the end rewarding, because Sheila found her life being enriched from sources she least expected. She no longer had only to give but could also receive and be refreshed, supported and instructed. There was a new sense of belonging to a community, as a kind of fluid and enlarging team.

Practical theology is done from below
The widely used slogan 'doing theology from below' has two connotations. Both of them reflect the perspective of liberation theology and its insistence on praxis. First, the reference is to theology's starting point. The cycle starts, as we have seen, with present experience which becomes questioned by some event or crisis. It starts in the concrete reality of where people are. This is the primary theological datum. Sheila started her voyage of discovery by being part of the life of the village and dealing with real people in their hurts and pains, joys and hopes. And this was the reality that all reflection and action had to address. The gospel had to be about their lives, building their community, standing by those people in their difficulties. Even the religious reaction gained credibility because it was about people's lives.

This is the heart of the praxis model. The term praxis points to the fact that all practice reflects the inner dynamic that informs it. So we have a two-stage pattern. Present practice has to be revealed with both its unrealities and falsehoods and also its inherent strengths, so that it can be challenged and changed. Out of the process comes a new praxis which, hopefully, enables creativity and growth. So Sheila and the congregation began to shake loose the myths about the function of the Chapel in the village, the family traditions and pietistic interpretations of the gospel. As they faced reality and began to accept some of the challenges of their Christian responsibility they could reformulate their beliefs and open up their practice. Yet they found they had not betrayed the past. Instead they discovered that in many ways they were recapturing the spirit of their founding parents and that faith was more real and personal than ever.

Secondly, however, working 'from below' means a 'preferential option for the poor'. The Church in liberation theology is rooted in a faith in God and an option for the poor. The suffering of the poor is a sign of everything that contradicts the will of God in history, for their suffering is not a matter of accident. It is in large part due to the way the world's resources are controlled.[5]

The poor are the standing sign of contradiction in the world. As those most sinned against, they demonstrate the presence of sin. Their hurt, rage or anxiety is the sign of injustice and oppression. The poor, the disadvantaged and the marginalized are those who receive grace in the midst of suffering and know it to be gospel. But the others, the powerful, the possessors, the secure, are not excluded. They, too, may suffer; but always they have a special responsibility to search for peace and justice.

Sheila, too, discovered the truth of the poor. From compassion for their plight she moved alongside them and learnt from them. It was also precisely the needs of poverty that made the whole situation real. For those on benefits or low wages a few pounds a month extra to be spent on fares could be crippling. Time wasted on public transport could be ill afforded. And the erosion of village life meant more to them – harder to shop, less to do, the search for work less and less possible – than those with cars and greater mobility. For Sheila the kind of village life worth saving became more about work and security than creating a rural retreat from the city. Through them she had begun to understand the crucifixion afresh, as well as the political dimension of salvation.

Practical theology is dialogue
The exploration and reflection stages of the pastoral cycle relate most closely to the critical correlation model. In many ways this is the 'boiler room' of practical theology, at least in its formal expression in academic and institutional contexts. Practical theology is essentially dialogic. That is, a number of elements are brought together into conversation with each other. We can see this clearly in the work of the study group on village life that Sheila gathered round herself. Their self-imposed task was to look at what was happening to their locality with a view to stimulating appropriate action. In order to do this a range of resources had to be tapped.

(i)   The actual situation needs to be charted, from land use to car ownership, from age profile to employment. To be done fully, various instruments of research have to be devised by someone who knows how, or can learn. Statistical information can be supported by more anecdotal material reflecting people's perceptions and opinions.

(ii) The broader scene is understood through pursuing various issues in the relevant literature, studying official and unofficial reports or inviting experts to meet the group. Thus the various social disciplines yield their varying and sometimes conflicting perspectives.

(iii) Then there is the identification of community resources: the skills available in the village and how appropriate they are; buildings and other community facilities; and the untapped human potential.

(iv) Finally there is the all-important question of beliefs and values. From a Christian point of view this is where explicit reference is made to faith. The tradition calls forth certain styles of commitment to ideals such as peace, justice, community, grace and salvation. There are resources in the Bible, prayer and worship and the wisdom of the saints and great teachers of the past which can guide and strengthen those caught up in contemporary issues. In an open situation this is set alongside other options, religious and humanistic.

There are in fact three discussions going on alongside each other, yet intertwined and influencing each other. There is first the attempt to make sense of the situation, to be aware of its strengths and weaknesses, its past and its prognosis. Secondly, there is the need to decide what to propose as the possible lines of action in the light of needs and resources. There is, thirdly, the critical but often neglected discussion of the value systems and assumptions that can and should inform every level of the process. Unfortunately this last often only tends to surface at points of controversy where there is open and perhaps polarized conflict. It should, however, be central to the agenda. Out of these various discussions comes the consensus that enables the group to take responsible decisions and to suggest action. For Sheila and many of her friends in the situation it was their faith that provided the basic warrant and dynamic for their participation.

This dialogic model is clearly exemplified in the work of Diocesan Social Responsibility Departments, especially in the production of reports on socio-economic issues. It is also very much the pattern found in academic practical theology. There the aim is to provide a grounding in the various disciplines on which practical theological reflection needs to draw, and in the more general introduction to skills and method. But it needs to be remembered that, however vital the process might be, it is only a part of the whole and, by itself, can be very abstract and remote. The constant academic temptation is to assume that reflection is action; that having written something or thought something the task has been completed. This is the criticism of the critical correlation approach by the liberationists: action is not seen to be a necessary consequence. Laurie Green points out that the pastoral cycle can be seen as two separate rather than interdependent halves:

> The dividing of the cycle into two is a constant and real danger, for many theologians have started out with every intention of completing the whole cycle but then have become so immersed in reflection they have forgotten to go to the action . . . Come to that, many parish churches fall for exactly this temptation and separate out their action from their theological reflection . . . [They] do their theological reflection on Sunday mornings but maybe do not even know the people who are involved with all the action that goes on during the rest of the week. This is anything but a united cycle of action and reflection.[6]

Practical theology draws on the tradition

There is a real tension here. Christian faith is rooted in the understanding of God as found in the person of Jesus. This tradition may be broad and diverse. But there is a real sense of givenness, of a faith 'once delivered to the saints' and passed on. Yet there has also to be a recognition that faith responds to and learns from the living present. One of the results of the dialogue is the discovery of new dimensions of faith and mission.

The applied theory model of practical theology obviously corresponds to the necessary element of givenness found in all mainstream Christian theology. It may be necessary to criticize the understanding of how theory relates to practice, but such a model at least safeguards the sense of tradition and revelation, the need to respect what the Bible or Church teaches. We do in fact live out of a continuity and we are truly given the treasures of wisdom from the past.

Tradition, however, has to be living. What comes down to us has itself been forged in the heat of controversy and practical reflection. There are certain nodal points which guide and inform tradition but, from the formation of the biblical texts to the present, tradition grows out of a dialogue between those foundational stories and events and the living present, illuminated by tradition. It is out of this that the gospel, as that which is proclaimed, becomes alive.

Sheila found this to be true when looking back over her experience. The tradition came to life precisely when it had ceased to be a chain, just at that point when forms of words could be abandoned and hallowed practices changed and freedom seized. It was then that the tradition came to be seen as that which was both precious and liberating. Learning about the history of the congregation, about those who despite persecution had started 'the cause', gave permission again to take initiatives with the underprivileged. And in doing that they found themselves closer to the cross and resurrection and could read Paul and John with new insight.

Practical theology informs spirituality
This point follows on from what has just been said. Sheila recognized in herself and in many others round her, a considerable change in Christian understanding. Church and world were less set apart. She treasured the insights of others as God's gifts. There was a new sensitivity to people. Politics were no longer alien. There was a new vitality to prayer and faith despite being overworked and tired. These and other things were now part of her and the fellowship she served. She could not read the Bible in any other way.

The pastoral cycle may move from experience through exploration and reflection to action. But there is more than one level at which it works. Perhaps the more obvious level of pragmatic activity is not so dominant as it appears. There is another, which is what is happening to people, their attitudes and expectations. Community work has always recognized that part of the process is 'people development' as a necessary component of community development.

This is an essential part of practical theology and is the burden of the habitus model. Theological activity cannot be separated from the life of faith, prayer and worship. The process of critical reflection and discovery is part of the pilgrimage of the people of God. This is true in the life of the congregation in the community. It is also true in the more formal context of academic study or structured enquiry.

> The suggestion, however, is not that we spin out of the practical, pastoral spiral into a new kind of abstract or personalistic spiritualization. It is to find spirituality in the concrete action and to live the action out of an historical spirituality. The correct relationship of prayer and action consists of prayer offered in the very process of liberation, when we experience an encounter with God **in our sisters and brothers**. Every great saint in history has managed this vital, concrete synthesis, and it has always constituted the secret of an authentically Christian life.[7]

Practical theology is a single activity

Sheila's experience was multi-faceted. She found herself working with distressed individuals, but she was also helping to form action groups around the school closure protest. She was concerned about the effects it was all having in particular cases but it was also necessary to understand the social and economic pressures that were bearing down on the community, changing it and challenging it. She was therefore working at several levels at once: from the micro-concerns of this or that person or family to the macro-issues of county and government policy. She had to draw on all her resources from training and experience. Even then it was an intense programme of listening and reading and enquiry; 'a steep learning curve'.

At the same time she was crossing other boundaries: between sacred and secular, Church and community. What was happening in the frenetic weeks of crisis spilled over into the life of the Christian community. It affected sermon preparation, both personal and corporate prayer, the shape of worship and the educational programme. It was no longer possible to work compartmentally. Every aspect of pastoral life was caught up in the cycle of action and reflection. It was here that Sheila began to recognize that what had been experienced in college as separate activities, preaching, teaching, liturgy and pastoral care, were not different things, each with their own rules, but aspects of the single call to faithful witness, service and obedience. The activism of pastoral and community work was sustained and given direction out of a rediscovered relevance of Bible and worship. The reflective reaching back into the tradition in study, sermon, prayer and sacrament became a voyage of discovery because of the questions that had been thrust on her. The pastoral cycle is a unifying force because it compels us to work out of the concrete reality in which God has placed us.[8]

Notes

1   Referred to in Green, Laurie, *Let's Do Theology* (Mowbray 1990), p. 24.

2   An example is *Faith in Leeds* (Leeds Council of Churches 1987).

3   Freire, Paulo, *Pedagogy of the Oppressed* (Penguin 1972).

4   Barbé, Dominique, 'Church Base Communities' in Cadorette, C. *et al.* (eds), *Liberation Theology – An Introductory Reader* (Orbis 1992), pp. 185–7.

5   Legge, Marilyn J., in Cadorette, op. cit., p. 165.

6   Green, op. cit., p. 39.

7   Boff, Leonardo, in Cadorette, op. cit., p. 238.

8   An alternative description of this unitary activity of practical theology has been proposed by Jeff Astley. In his book *Ordinary Theology* (Ashgate 2002) he employs the phrase to describe the theology and theologizing of Christians who have received little or no theological education, but is the theology which forms the basic Christian thinking of most members of the Church. This is an approach which comes nearest to the 'habitus' model of practical theology but does not consciously draw on theological methods such as the pastoral cycle.

Chapter 7

Learning from experience

We turn now to examine the various stages of the pastoral cycle to see how they operate in practice. The first stage involves taking experience seriously as the point of departure for the ministry and mission of the Church. We have been making the case in previous chapters that this seriousness is theological and not merely an exercise in pastoral common sense. We are maintaining that theological issues are latent in the specific contours of every situation in ministry, and that if they are explored thoughtfully we have here a way of doing theology which is available to every Christian. We may in fact enter the pastoral cycle at any point, but the easiest way to demonstrate its effectiveness is by starting with concrete experience.

In the first part of this chapter we will use three particular situations in ministry as a series of touchstones for the process of learning from experience and moving towards appropriate action.

(A) When a new minister arrives in a local church she is usually well advised to listen very hard and initiate nothing for a considerable period. She has to attend closely to the whole context and content of the church's ministry before shaping some understanding of what is really going on here, and what might be helpful strategies to discuss with the church's continuing leadership. She needs to learn from experience.

(B) The youth leader comes out of a bruising session with the youth group. He needs to talk to his fellow leaders and to think hard about what went wrong on this occasion. Only when they have thoroughly raked through the ashes of the session and spread out the factors before each other, can they presume to bring forward other elements of their faith, and their knowledge of good youth work practice, in order to plan a different approach next time. They have learned from experience.

(C) A thorough review of worship is under way. The ministry team have all sorts of dissatisfactions and ideas, but they decide first of all to do a survey among the congregation to see what the feeling is at grass roots. 'And why not include those who just come very occasionally, or not at all,' says one member of the team, 'to see what puts them off?' They want to learn from experience.

The key elements of learning from experience

In none of these situations, however, will the people involved automatically learn from what has happened. The learning process has to be deliberate; otherwise they are condemned to repeating the past. Any attempt to learn from the actualities of pastoral experience will involve at least three processes:

- gathering information and attending to experience
- recording information and experience
- shaping information and experience for presentation.

Gathering information and attending to experience
We will examine the practicalities of gathering such information later in the chapter, but at the outset something must be said about the style of the student or minister who is trying to do justice to the particularities of the situation. The heart of the process lies in giving that situation a total attentiveness, much as the heart of listening in pastoral ministry is also about unambiguous attention. It is a commonplace of counselling theory that three dispositions are necessary in the listener if the client is truly to be heard.[1]

Genuineness. As in counselling, so in attending to experience in ministry, there needs to be an honesty of interest and engagement. Simply playing with a few tricks of the trade, with feigned interest and seriousness, will undermine the whole process. In example (A) above, if the new minister has already worked out her blueprint for the church, it will become obvious either at the supposed information gathering stage or when the strategy which emerges bears no relationship to the facts, stories and ideas she was given by church members.

Respect. An attitude of respect is demonstrated when the person gathering the information maintains an openness and humility which does not seek to diminish, label or manipulate the facts and stories which emerge, but rather to hear the information with the care and respect it deserves. He is not in a position to judge its accuracy or wisdom just yet. He must hear it first and take it seriously. The youth worker in example (B) must hear precisely how his colleagues perceived the disastrous session, and not be afraid to recall and name the reaction of the group in all its painfulness.

Accurate empathy. Just as a counselling client needs the reassurance that her problem is being understood before she will entrust more of the issue to the listener, so in understanding a situation in ministry, a student or minister will need to enter into the realities, thoughts and feelings before him, and as far as possible, experience them from within. Then the situation is likely to carry on delivering itself up to the empathic engagement of the listener. In example (C) the congregation being consulted about worship needs to know that their feelings and reactions are genuinely understood. The ministry team will then be known to have done its best to 'see it their way', and a basis of trust will have been established for the future development of a strategy for renewing the church's worship. It is also widely accepted in counselling that two further skills are needed to supplement these fundamental attitude skills.[2]

Listening to the bass-line. In pastoral care this means listening to the 'body language' of the person to see if another story is being told at this more instinctive level, which complements or conflicts with the surface-telling of the story. In terms of listening to a situation rather than a person, it means looking out for the 'sub-text' which may be present. The new minister may discern a deep spiritual malaise in the church or a power struggle going on between elements in the church with different operational theologies.[3] Our youth group leader may hear beneath the events of that session a deeper frustration at how young people are being treated by the church. Our ministry team may begin to be aware of a different issue surfacing through the responses of the congregational survey – a concern about styles of leadership or a perceived continual desire for change for its own sake.

Listening to oneself. A counsellor learns to listen to her own responses when working with a client. Those responses might give an important clue as to why other significant people in the client's story have reacted as they have done, or why the client herself feels so completely trapped. So, in listening to other ministerial experiences and situations the thoughtful practitioner will not just listen open-mouthed to the situation as given, but will be listening to her own reactions, not in order to pre-empt evaluation at a later stage, but in order to understand the depth of passion aroused by proposed changes in worship, or the apparent anger of certain sections of the minister's new church as they re-tell significant moments in the church's story.

What these attitudes amount to is a stance of 'critical openness' to the information or experience under review. Just as much as persons in distress, situations are capable of yielding their particular complex contours when attended to with due care. Another analogy is that used by Edward Farley who writes of a 'hermeneutic of situations' to put alongside a hermeneutic of texts.[4] Situations in ministry need to be read with the same subtlety as sacred texts; the skills may be different, but the needs are similar if interpretation is to be accurate.

Recording information and experience
Again we will look at the practicalities of recording later in the chapter, but what we can usefully do now is note some principles of recording which should lie behind particular practices.

Accessibility. Twenty pages of random notes, statistics and ideas, presented on assorted pieces of paper without subheadings, will seem much more threatening to a student's supervisor, or subsequently much less useful to the student himself, than something half that length but ordered and coherent. Our new minister should record impressions under particular headings, e.g. 'key past events', 'dreams', 'conflicts', 'skills', or under names of individuals and organizations.

Quantity. There is no end to information gathering. Only connect, and we discover that everything is linked to everything else in ministry. Good research methods require clear boundaries to be drawn around the particular material which is of closest relevance to the task. The ministry team in our example does not need to gather data on the congregation's views on worship ten years ago, but on the other hand they may well be interested in what peripheral members of the church think of the current provision of worship, as well as more committed members. The boundaries need to be drawn realistically around what information is actually significant.

Availability. There is no point in pursuing to the death information which is clearly either unavailable or lost under the dust of impossibly obscure archives. Only the probability of vast pecuniary gain ought to call for such heroism!

Professional resources. There is again no point in labouring to re-invent the wheel of research methods. If, for instance, a questionnaire is needed which requires some degree of sophistication, a friendly local sociologist may be able to help. A genuinely useful questionnaire is actually much more difficult to produce than most people think. The Open University produces excellent material on information gathering, recording and analysis (see Bibliographies).

Shaping information and experience
If the information thus gathered and recorded is to be of any further use it has to be shaped to be ready for presentation. That presentation may be to a supervisor who is going to work on it with a student, or it may be material from a church audit which has to be made available to the main church meeting. Or it may simply be that the information and experience has to be useful and comprehensible for the new minister for future reference and reflection, or for the student who has later to write a report on a long placement. In any of these cases, time has to be spent giving shape to all the material collected. This will mean making connections, weeding out irrelevant material, drawing up headings, making charts and graphs, amending maps and writing up notes.

In some cases the experience and information is shaped by the requirement of reports for a training institution. There may be a standard report form for self-assessment or supervisor assessment, and a number of other standard forms will be referred to later. The point to note here is that time given to ordering and shaping raw material is rarely wasted. The greater danger is that unshaped material is so wild and woolly that it is lost, avoided or forgotten.

We have now, therefore, identified the three key elements of learning from experience: gathering, recording and shaping information and experience. The rest of this chapter will concentrate on two particular contexts where the process of learning from experience is the central task: student placements and church audits.

Student learning through placements

Term-time and vacation placements, some as short as two weeks, some as long as eighteen months, are bread-and-butter, core elements of most forms of theological education for ministry.[5] They serve many purposes: they keep students earthed in the realities of pastoral ministry when the lecture room threatens to take over their fading vision; they provide the laboratory where methods of relating theory and practice can be tested and refined; they broaden the spectrum of students' experience of ministry; they introduce a practitioner's wisdom to the central task of theological reflection.

At the heart of the enterprise, however, they offer a controlled framework for learning from experience and practising the methods which, in adapted form, can sustain a lifetime of thoughtful ministry. The actual recording methods below are not in themselves likely to be used regularly in active ministry, but the value of them in training is that they slow up the learning cycle in such a way that the process is laid bare, and it is that process, rather than the particular methods themselves, which has to become second nature for effective, theologically informed ministry.

We will assume that a placement has been set up by negotiation between the training institution, the student, the supervisor, and a particular context for ministry. All four parties have their respon-sibilities, and the relationship between them is crucial to effective learning. That relationship is well explored in Foskett and Lyall's *Helping the Helpers*. The purpose of this chapter, however, is to describe some of the strategies for digging into the experience and recording it, rather than to examine the task of supervision and theological reflection (see Chapter 9). What follows are some of the well-tried methods of getting under the surface of the experience and recording it in retrievable form.

Diary. The simplest and most effective way of recording impressions, encounters and ideas is the humble diary. At its simplest the diary gives an opportunity for noting the external events, facts and structures of the parish. The student can record conversations and people's interests, and note how the staff of the church conduct their meetings, how decisions are made, what plans are afoot and how involved lay people are in ministry. The student may also note down the sights and smells of the area, the impressions he got from walking down the High Street and from stepping inside the church buildings.

A further use of the diary is for recording the inner journey the student is making, a journey which may be made up of observations, hunches, instinctive reactions, and spiritual responses. There may be questions, some of which may not be answered or even be answerable in the course of the placement. There may be tentative explorations of the distribution of power or the tensions existing between different models of mission. The diary may contain quotes or anecdotes which seem to express larger truths about the church. Some students may write poetry or prayers in their diary. All is grist to the mill of experiential learning. To read such a diary later is to enter a vital narrative which by its very nature as a document of experiences, fragments and personal responses, provides a primary source of material for reflection.

Community profile. An early task in a placement should be the building up of a community profile so that the student can place the activities of the church in the broader context of the life of the area. A sample form may be found in Appendix A. The first thing to do is to go for a walk. No amount of research in libraries and files can be a substitute for that primary encounter with the area that comes from wandering the streets, watching, listening and experiencing first-hand the kaleidoscope of sensations which any community offers.

When the place has begun to take on a character of its own in the student's mind, then it becomes important to know about population numbers, age, wealth, types of housing, car ownership, employment, ethnic groups, etc. Such information is usually available in the main library or Town Hall in the Small Area Statistics for each 2001 Census Enumeration District. Such information is also easily available on the National Census 2001 website under Neighbourhood Statistics. The disadvantage is that there is not always anyone to hand from whom to seek advice or help in the interpretation of the data. Other material for the community profile may take longer to compile since it may ask questions about social problems, tensions in the community, or how the community views the church. Longer exposure to the locality will be needed to uncover the deeper currents within it, with lots of listening and careful observation. Contrast this with what most clergy find themselves having to do on arrival in a new church; they are pitched into the centre of a community within a community, with hardly a chance to stand back and get the broader picture. The immediate is all-demanding, and most churches provide the new minister with more than enough pressing problems! However, that time of first impressions and information gathering will never come again.

Church profile. Another important profile to build up in the early days of a placement is that of the church and its membership. A sample form for an Anglican parish is found in Appendix B. Such a profile allows the student to gain a bird's eye view of the congregation, details of which she can then engage with more closely. Some information is purely factual: How many people go to church? Where do they live? What social background do they come from? Other information would be more about forms of ministry, by whom it is exercised and what training is offered. Other information again might be about church structures, plans and partnerships.

On the basis of this material the student can then begin to ask more informed questions. For example, she can investigate why the congregation seems to be so solidly middle class and to be making so little impact on the former council estate. Is it to do with styles of worship and ministry, or a long tradition of social and emotional distance? Is it complicated by the church's rigorist baptism policy? What do the people on the estate actually feel about the church now (as opposed to ten years ago), and what do those in the church actually feel about the estate and the church's failure to make any impact?

A church profile also enables the bigger questions to be raised for longer-term answering. What model of mission is dominant, and how does leadership operate? How does the church handle change and conflict? Where does power really lie? One can even begin to address the theological questions which always underlie church structures and processes: What understanding of God is operative? What model of authority? What picture of the Kingdom of God? A church profile is an indispensable tool for understanding the dynamics of a congregation and then planning an appropriate strategy for church life.

Significant event sheet (Appendix C). Regularly in Christian ministry we experience events which have the potential to disturb, puzzle or excite us; events which raise important issues for theology and ministry, and indeed for society as a whole. It might be an encounter with a homeless man on the doorstep, or a conversation with a thoroughly secularized young mother at the school gate. On another occasion it was a young Christian called Brian who sold newspapers on a city street and had a remarkable pastoral ministry among the city's misfits. What had we to learn from his eccentric ministry? Or there was the man who spoke about his temptation to commit suicide because he was accused of molesting a child; a few days later he killed himself. What could we have done differently? Another time we launched a new branch of the World Development Movement in town and went to lobby our MP. With smooth words and fine phrases he promised little. What political lessons could we learn?

A significant event sheet records the incident and starts to analyse the factors contributing to its outworking in an ordered and disciplined way. It also allows for preliminary theological reflection on the event. Further analysis and reflection come later in the learning cycle, but in the quiet at the end of the day the student begins to wrestle with the psychological, social and theological complexity of some particular event, and his observation and analysis are sharpened for further encounters.

Pastoral focus. A student may be asked to choose a person, a family, a group or an institution with whom he will do more work and reflection in the course of a placement. The aim is similar to that for the significant event, to sensitize the student to the subplots of pastoral situations and to practise the skills of thoughtful pastoral action. The difference lies in the extended nature of the interaction and the fact that the pastoral focus is deliberately chosen rather than being a fortuitous event. The same style of recording sheet may be used, or a longer report written.

Verbatim. This is a well-proven method of recording a particular interview or pastoral encounter, as nearly as possible word for word. It needs to be done by the student immediately after the interview and due account taken of the inevitable filters which will distort the student's memory. It does however provide a very useful source of material for subsequent discussion with an experienced practitioner or supervisor. Typically, the verbatim account will start with an introduction, stating what the student knew about the person before the conversation took place, and how the encounter came about. It will then move on to as accurate a record of the conversation as possible, phrase by phrase; and it will then have a section on evaluation in which the student attempts to identify what was really going on, what expectations and feelings were around, what could have been done or said more helpfully, and what to learn from the whole experience. The whole verbatim is then ready as raw material for a supervision session.[6] We will return to the process of theological reflection on this material in Chapter 9.

Personal reaction sketch. Towards the end of a piece of field education this can be a preliminary attempt to shape the experiences of the placement into a form useful for the process of learning. The questions are deliberately innocent and open (see Appendix D) but the type of answers given will be significant. What was your initial impression of the church? What have you found most difficult to cope with? What do you think are the frustrations of ministry in this church? What are the main things you have learnt about yourself? If answers are attempted while still on the placement or just afterwards, the experiences will be fresh and the responses will smell authentic, which makes them a valuable, scarce resource in subsequent reflection with a tutor.

Sermon evaluation sheet. This method of recording is different from those above in that it is not done by the student. Naturally, it is done by listeners to the student, and the more the better. Sermon appraisal is given to students in many different ways in training institutions, often by video and discussion, or peer group appraisal after actual services. On placements there is the special opportunity to involve a considerable number of people from the congregation, many of whom will have heard thousands of sermons over the years and never before been able to offer an ordered critique, so far beyond feedback is the ordinary preacher! The example of a sermon evaluation form reproduced in Appendix E gives the listener the opportunity to react to both content and delivery. Such innocent questions as 'What was the aim of the sermon?' may evoke responses which are the despair of preachers, but better that they should know this is the confusion caused, rather than assume for thirty years that their delivery is as clear as the Ten Commandments. This is an exercise to enter into with humility.

The church audit

St Saviour and the Holy Family was proud of its past. There was, indeed, a strong 'family' feel about it. It wasn't just that four or five actual families seemed to crop up everywhere in its life, but everyone else seemed to know each other as well, and genuinely to care if someone wasn't at church on Sunday. They were missed. There were a good number of children too, not as many as in the early 1960s, of course; then the Sunday School teachers numbered 22 in all, including Helen Nugget who was known to be a little bit simple, but good-hearted, and she always gave the crayons out.

The trouble was that the 'family' seemed to be dwindling. Nothing to be alarmed about of course, but it was many months since a new family had come to church and in the meantime some had died, others moved away, and others simply seemed to be coming less regularly. And then there was Tony. Tony and his wife Kate were rather on the strident side, some people thought, always reminding the church about the single men's hostel up the road, and the number of children out on the streets at all hours, and the church's failure to relate to its community. All in all the time seemed right to have what the bishop called an 'audit', a taking-stock-and-planning process. Alf, the churchwarden, said it couldn't do any harm.

The vicar of St Saviour and the Holy Family was Bob Robinson ('I'm more like an elder brother,' he said, using the over-worked 'family' category again). He called a meeting of the Parochial Church Council on a Wednesday – not a good night he was told: 'There's football on't telly' – but they met anyway. Opinions were mixed. Why spend a lot of time finding out what's going on when they all knew what's going on, and why plan what to do when they all knew what to do? They just had to do it better. Bob, however, believed it would be a useful exercise, and the family of the church might be drawn closer together. So they said yes, unanimously in the end, although there was a suspicion Greta was asleep at the time – or had just left her knitting needle pointing upwards.

That was **Step One: Decision** – making sure there was a positive, informed decision to go ahead with the project, which will take a lot of the church's time and energy.

Bob was charged to go away with the churchwardens and do

some preliminary thinking to bring back to the PCC next time. Bob got hold of a diocesan pack on parish audits,[7] and one wet Friday night they settled down to some basic questions. Should there be a co-ordinating group? (Yes.) How many members? (Not too many – perhaps six.) Should it be a short, sharp audit, or a longer, more leisurely one? (Short and sharp – we're good at pitching in for special tasks. Remember when . . . ?) Should we have a consultant – what Alf called a 'know-it-all'? (Yes – useful for keeping the group on the rails and helping it to see what it might be missing.) And so a basic structure was formulated, ready for the next PCC.

The PCC was in a beneficent mood. (No football, and the Spring Fayre had gone surprisingly well.) All the recommendations were accepted, and the Council even drew up a list of those people it felt should be on the co-ordinating group. A wise choice, thought Bob, with a good mix of age, experience of church life and social background. They even included Ian, whom Bob regarded as his 'friendly sceptic' on the edge of things. The *coup de grâce* was a decision to invite Tony, Tony of the radical commitments, to chair the group.

The co-ordinating group got under way. Tony wisely spent some time having the group explore its expectations and special interests, and he even asked people to identify their blind spots. ('God,' said Ian, the friendly sceptic.) They decided on a working strategy, a timetable, different groups which would be needed for different tasks, special skills in the congregation which might be useful, how they would go back to the church with their findings. It looked good.

That was **Step Two: Preparation** – setting up a key co-ordination group and not rushing the process of getting the framework right, and accepted by the main participants.

Not surprisingly, Tony suggested the first task should be to work on an audit of the local community. Everyone agreed because they could see that an audit which started with the church would end with the church. (For a group from St Saviour and the Holy Family to start outside their own immediate life was the first small miracle that occurred in this audit. It was not the last.) They set up three sub-groups for this part of the exercise: one to work on a comprehensive map, one to search out local statistics and facts about the community, and one to research people's attitudes to their community. The map group was quickly into action. On the largest scale map they could get they marked boundaries, places of worship and of education, major meeting places ('Don't forget the Labour Party office,' said Tony), hospitals and social service centres, industry, and much more. They marked different types of housing in different colours and spent much time digging out the addresses of a host of voluntary bodies they had hardly even heard of.

The statistics group felt they were home and dry after they discovered the Neighbourhood section of the National Census website. Peter found that a lot of this information could be selectively printed off. Some further surfing uncovered even more material about organizations and people in his community. It was a fascinating but complex task, pulling out the facts they wanted for the precise area of the parish, and there were a lot of conversations that started 'Did you realize that . . . ?' They also went to the Planning Office, the Social Services department and a number of other bodies, following up reports they remembered the local paper had said had been published. The Citizens' Advice Bureau was especially helpful. 'Fancy all that information being right there next to Safeways,' said Greta, 'and I thought it was all about family planning!'

The third group, working on people's attitudes, had a more difficult job. They wanted to know what people thought and felt about their community. They decided to use a mixture of questionnaires and 'chatting around'. They got the questionnaires into youth clubs and OAP clubs, women's groups and PTAs, ethnic groups and doctors' surgeries; just wherever they could. Sometimes they managed to run a session with a particular group and discuss what they really meant; those discussions were extremely lively, especially when the OAPs discussed the new bus timetables. The questionnaire itself focused on what people felt were the good and bad points about their community, where there was conflict and who held the power. What groups in the community were working effectively for change? Was it a consulting community, respectful of others? What were its needs? And what about values and beliefs, right and wrong, God and the Church? (It was important here not to 'load' the questions but to let people answer in their own terms.)

Kate had a valuable idea which came out of her work at the local FE College. She got a group of her students to spend every Wednesday afternoon going around chatting to different people, asking the same kind of question as in the survey but in a more informal way. They talked to people at bus stops, lunch clubs and school gates; they talked to old people with wonderful memories – one girl talked to her grandmother seriously for the first time ever, and loved it; one or two of them were clever enough to see the need to talk to people in the pub! Together they came up with a composite picture of attitudes which was fascinating in its breadth and richness, and full of insight, peppered with wonderful quotes and anecdotes.

That was **Step Three: Community** – embarking on a thorough investigation of the resources and needs of the local community in which the church's mission is set.

The pace was hotting up. The time had come to look at the church. 'Home territory,' said Alf. 'Much safer.' But was it? The groups set up to explore the church's resources and needs were determined not to relax their critical observation or to apply 'sticking plasters' where the church was wounded. Again there was a group working on a map, this time of where church members lived; and not only members of St Saviour's, but of every Christian denomination – different colours for different churches. Gaining the co-operation of the other churches was a crucial exercise; Bob and Tony did that between them. Interesting patterns began to emerge: quite a lot of the church's leadership lived outside the parish; the Methodists were particularly strong in the former council estate where St Saviour's had hardly anyone; Ian the friendly sceptic was surrounded by Christian families ('Now I understand why the cat says grace before meals,' he said).

Another group was doing a very impressive job on church facts and statistics. A tame statistician had a field day with membership figures, baptisms, Easter communicants, financial trends, average giving, yearly donations to charity and so on. Funerals were booming but weddings were plummeting ('It's something in the water,' said Greta). Others were looking at buildings, their own and others, thinking about their suitability and adaptability, opportunities for joint use and development. People looked at the ministry of the church, the place of women in leadership, the participation of children, committee structures, worship patterns and ecumenism. The material was fascinating – and prolific.

As in the community audit, a third group was tackling the attitudes of the congregation with a questionnaire which had the

same issues as the community survey (comparisons were important), but also a host of other questions about background, how
they first got involved, what other organizations they belonged to,
as well as what annoyed them about the church and what they
wanted changing. There was much debate about how this survey
was to be handled: given out at church? filled in at church?
interview at home? for fringe members also, and if so, how big is a
fringe? They decided on a mixed economy, but still had to work
hard to get a comprehensive return.[8]

That was **Step Four: Church** – initiating a thorough audit of
the church, its resources and potential.

After three months of hard and very stimulating work, the co-
ordinating group considered it had the information it wanted to
present. The working groups had submitted their material and it
now had to be shaped for presentation to the church. It needed to
be concise, clear and imaginative; the interminable listing of
endless statistics would achieve less than nothing; it would be
counterproductive. The group then spent three weeks putting
together a programme for a Sunday conference of the church
family ('And anyone else who wants to come,' said Alf, this representing the second miracle of the audit). The day started with
worship and then, after coffee, the major presentation began.
Through a PowerPoint presentation that projected charts, maps,
statistics, by taped interviews, by short résumé talks and a variety
of speakers, through anecdotes and humour, old photos and new
town plans, the story was told. Over lunch a display of statistics
and charts, pictures and graphs was there to be perused; everywhere conversation was animated. After lunch the presentation
had to be completed, and everyone received a full pack of
information, the report itself, colour-coded and digestible. Now
was the time to respond . . .

That was **Step Five: Presentation** – making the presentation
to the church and community in as vivid a way as possible, giving
people material to take away both in their hands and in their
hearts.

The audit then proceeded through the steps which go further
than this chapter intends. We have been concentrating on gathering, recording and shaping information and experience so that
the church can learn from it and adapt its mission accordingly.
It's worth noting, however, that the hard work of personal and
institutional change is only just beginning at this point. The rest of

the day was spent reflecting on all that the audit was saying to the church in the light of its understanding of the gospel and what that meant in terms of mission in that locality. Out of that day came a PCC day-away and a series of groups addressing various areas of the church's life. A programme of renewal emerged which was in effect a five-year plan, and the consultant was asked to stay in touch to help them at key moments and to monitor their progress.

This was **Step Six: Reflection** – exploring the findings of the audit in the light of Christian thinking about Church and community (see Bibliography).

The task of this chapter properly stops at this point, or indeed before it. We have been presenting here an example of learning from experience as represented by the church audit. The processes of reflection, and moving from reflection to action, belong to later chapters. For completeness, however, let us note the other stages of the audit:

Step Seven: Planning – drawing up an action plan for the church and having it owned by the decision-making body.

Step Eight: Review – building in periodic reviews to monitor progress and initiate variations in the church's strategy according to the leading of the Spirit.

It would be good to complete the story, so this is what happened! Interestingly, people were profoundly changed by the audit in St Saviour and the Holy Family. Tony was heard to say: 'There's more honest faith in this church than I ever realized.' Bob said it had rejuvenated his ministry. Greta now works a day a week in the Citizens' Advice Bureau. Ian the friendly sceptic said, 'I've got to take my hat off to this church – and maybe to God!' He now goes to Parish Communion each week. And at the opening of the day centre and lunch club in the church rooms, Alf said, 'We want this place not just to serve its own little church family, but to be available for the whole community.' And that was the third miracle that came out of the church audit. This church, which had started by defining itself in terms of an introverted model of Church and Kingdom, had discovered a breadth of engagement within the gospel which had taken them by enjoyable surprise. The 'family' was no longer 'those of us who go to church', but the whole community, as loved by God and called into new life and hope. The church had been involved in a profound exercise in learning from experience.

That indeed has been the theme of this chapter: that learning from experience is a fundamental method in ministry. It is a deliberate and purposeful activity, calling for comprehensive gathering, accurate recording, and skilful shaping of information and experience. We have offered two particular examples of the method, in student placements and church audits. The next stage in the pastoral cycle is to engage in a systematic exploration of the situation under review, using the appropriate tools of analysis.

Notes

1   Truax, C.B. and Carkhuff, R.R., *Towards Effective Counselling and Psychotherapy Training and Practice* (Aldine Press 1967).

2   A good exposition of basic listening skills is to be found in Jacobs, M., *Swift to Hear* (SPCK 1985).

3   A helpful analysis of different operational theologies of the Church is contained in Dulles, A., *Models of the Church* (Gill and Macmillan 1988) (2nd edition).

4   The idea of a 'hermeneutic of situations' is developed in Farley, E., *Theologia* (Fortress Press 1983). See Bibliography for Chapter 5.

5   Field education has long been part of theological education, but it has experienced significant milestones, for example in the embedding of pastoral studies in the ACCM syllabus in 1979, and in two important Church of England studies, *Education for the Church's Ministry* in 1987 and *Theology in Practice* in 1988 (both ACCM/ABM publications).

6   For a more comprehensive account of this method, see Foskett, John and Lyall, David, *Helping the Helpers* (SPCK 1989), p. 139.

7   A reliable form of audit is produced by Faithworks (details on website). Others are produced by, for example, the Evangelical Urban Training Project and denominational bodies.

8   The best introduction to a narrative approach to congregational life is to be found in Hopewell, J., *Congregation: Stories and Structures* (SCM 1988). See also Bibliography.

Chapter 8

Inter-disciplinary working

The second stage of the pastoral cycle is exploration: that is, assessing and analysing the situation we are looking at in the light of all the information available. Practical theology is essentially dialogic. It draws into mutual conversation those theoretical and practical disciplines which can help the processes of understanding and reflection, such as the social sciences, theology, philosophy, literature, and other fields of learning and practice. But this puts practical theology on the frontiers, and often it simply is not very comfortable living on these boundaries, apparently belonging nowhere and being pushed in different directions. The practical theologian has to sustain this tension.

In this chapter we want to look at this aspect of practical theology, as a discipline living on the boundaries and creating dialogue and meeting.[1] This is a situation of great creative opportunity as well as of tensions and pitfalls. The theme will be taken up in two ways. First, the inter-disciplinary nature of practical theology in an academic sense. In exploring the human condition use is made of all the human sciences as well as other fields of knowledge. This issue is especially important in relation to more formal situations such as study groups and working parties, academic classes and research. Secondly, attention will be given to the inter-professional context of practical theology. Here the focus is more clearly on the pastoral activity of the minister alongside other caring professions.

Practical theology as an inter-disciplinary task

Arthur, minister of the local Free Church congregation, has been asked to call on Peter and Jean, two of his members. He is puzzled as to what it might be about although he has noticed certain signs of strain in the family. When he arrives the conversation turns to anxieties they have over their teenage children, Mary (aged 15) and Tom (aged 13). It appears that the school is reporting some fall-off in the children's work and even suspicions of some antisocial behaviour. Mary is becoming shy and withdrawn, while Tom has become aggressive. At once Arthur begins to explore different lines of possible causes through asking open-ended but relevant questions. Clearly issues of adolescent development are around. It may be, as they say, 'a phase'. But Arthur senses something more and so he enquires about the family situation. Suddenly it all begins to come out. Peter has lost his job, made redundant without warning. Jean is still working but of course money is now very tight. Peter finds it very hard to accept that it is not his fault, feels let down by life, and bereft of purpose and status. He is going through all the stages of anger and low self-esteem as applications are turned down. Meanwhile they try to keep up appearances. No one in church knows, for instance, even though they are a family well integrated into the life of the community. The family is having to take all the strain and it is coming out emotionally in Mary and Tom's behaviour.

In order to deal with such a situation Arthur has to have some appreciation not only of human growth and development and family dynamics but of the psychology of work and redundancy. Moreover, in order to help Peter see his situation more dispassionately so that he does not need to feel personally belittled, Arthur has to be aware of national economic patterns as they impinge on the situation. He has to help Peter find the way around the benefits system and where help can be obtained. He also has to be aware of Jean's situation as a mother, wife, woman and now the only breadwinner.

In other words, a single pastoral case is linked directly or indirectly with a myriad dimensions of life, from the personal to the national, from the individual to the intricate structure of complex social institutions. How can Arthur be expected to cope? He cannot know everything or be an expert in everything. Yet it is important, not only to know the limitations of one's competence and to turn to others for help, but also to be constantly and grow-ingly aware of many aspects of life, and the theories and insights that are found in disciplines other than one's own.

Arthur also has a son, Jimmy, who is at theological college, training for the ministry. It is an intensive three-year course, including a good amount of time in field work. Jimmy is coming to the end of his course and is beginning to realize that time is running out. There simply is not enough time for everything that is obviously important in preparation for the pastoral task. More-over he is discovering that it is all more complex and demanding than he could ever have dreamed. If it is true that he has only just begun to scratch the surface of theology, imagine how it must be with the sociology and psychology and other social sciences. All that has been possible in the time available has been a smattering of an introduction in a limited number of fields.

Arthur and Jimmy are sensitive and wise. At least they accept that, even if the ideal is unobtainable, it is necessary to take other fields of knowledge seriously; and that they are as diverse and controversial as theology itself. Both know colleagues and friends who are either content to remain ignorant and to reflect current popular prejudices or who act out of superficial knowledge obtained from the newest fad in the subject, popularized on television.

Exploring the pastoral situation must draw on the insights of many disciplines. The practical theologian, then, is found in dia-logue with many areas of knowledge. The old adage 'Jack of all trades, master of none' carries with it a sense of disapproval, of someone who flits from one area to another and cannot surely be other than a dilettante or bumbling amateur. This is an accusation that must be taken seriously. If practical theology is to enjoy any respect it must be seen not only to take the risks of being inter-disciplinary but it must also be prepared to work at its task in a responsible and rigorous manner.

The pressure is that of having to get on with the job; the danger therefore is of being superficial. In the 'academy' there are other constraints: the demands of an almost impossibly wide syllabus in a limited amount of time. Even in research it is not always possi-ble to cover the interlocking fields as well as desired. The tempta-tion is to give up and be satisfied with the second-hand. But that is a counsel of despair; it is better to strive constantly towards a greater competence. Meanwhile it is important to be on guard

against the traps and pitfalls so that they may be avoided when-
ever possible.

It is important also to underline and emphasize the virtue of
inter-disciplinary working. We live at a time of exponential growth
in knowledge in many fields. It is said that expertise is 'to know
more and more about less and less'. Specializations multiply
almost as we watch. The threat is fragmentation of knowledge and
lack of communication between disciplines. What is needed is
the courage to make connections and to see things as a whole.
Inter-disciplinary dialogue has become a necessity. Moreover it is
recognized that creative insights often come precisely at those
places where disciplines overlap or challenge each other. There is,
therefore, no need to be ashamed to be living at the boundaries, in
however lowly a way. Maybe the practical theologian has to
endure the risk of marginalization, ridicule and error but he or
she can also be at the place of the new possibility, discovery and
prophecy.

However, three cautions need to be heeded in inter-disciplinary work:

Keeping up to date
This is very difficult in one subject field, let alone across a
number. But it is not good enough to be content with a smattering of information gathered in a course taken twenty years ago or
gathered from the latest popular paperback. All fields are changing and growing. In every discipline there are different schools
of thought and clashes of interpretation. It is important, for
example, to be aware of some of the main types of counselling
techniques from the humanistic to the behaviourist; or to recognize the differences between Marx, Weber and Durkheim or the
different protagonists in the secularization debate in the sociology
of religion.

It may well be true that the practical theologian will have to rely
more on secondary sources than may be desirable. But there are
usually accessible recent surveys of progress in particular fields
and there is always a continuous stream of basic textbooks being
published. While being aware of how many fields are potentially
involved, it is good practice to develop something of a specialization in one or two relevant areas. To be competent in one particular area can mean that we are more aware that other areas are
equally diverse and complex.

Pastoral pragmatism

A further danger for the practitioner is that of a too simple pastoral pragmatism. The practical theologian, lay or ordained, works under pressure and has to decide priorities. This will usually mean that those things which occupy the attention of the practitioner at present will dictate the direction he or she takes. That is both reasonable and natural. But it too has its dangers.

First, there is the danger of being dictated to by the pastoral situation. A woman can present marital problems which the pastor can take at face value. But it may be that a wider perspective is needed to overcome the limitations of the presenting problems. There may for instance be a possibility of abuse or a cultural factor hidden in the story. It is important, therefore, for the pastor to be deepening and broadening the resources from which to work.

Similarly, most pastors will have certain skills and experience, but these may be very limited and at times unsuitable. There has to be an awareness that other approaches and perspectives may be worth considering. It is no use, for instance, approaching all loss on the basis of grief, relevant as that may usually be.

Perhaps the greatest danger is what Pattison calls 'a cheerful eclectic approach'. Like a magpie, the practitioner gathers jewels from various quarters, wherever they happen to catch the eye. There is every reason to use a tool that appears to work. But it is something else to suggest that this is the last word on the matter. There are those involved in ministry who seem to be susceptible to the blandishments of those selling the latest school of thought, taking it up with uncritical enthusiasm. Moreover, the eclectic person may bring together a bizarre collection of bits and pieces that simply do not fit together. It is not good enough to say: 'I use what appeals to me.'

An example of this approach can be found in some of the Church Growth literature. The storehouses of anthropology, sociology, social psychology and group dynamics have here been raided to suggest how and why church growth can occur. But there is sometimes, especially in some more popular, 'hands-on' material, no reference to alternative understandings nor any critical analysis of the material used. The result is sometimes a two-dimensional view of human existence which is being treated to a pseudo-behaviourist theory, which is itself really a form of mechanistic technology. The point is not that we should not

undertake such a study, nor that many results are not interesting
and useful, but that there is need of a much greater awareness of
the limitations of the work done. It is impossible to elevate what
can be valuable insights into a comprehensive theory without
critical reserve.

False assimilation

The inter-disciplinary dialogue at the heart of practical theology
can be challenging and exciting, opening up all kinds of rich
possibilities. The most important aspect of this dialogue, of course,
is between theology and its partners, mainly in the social sciences.
It is on this dialogue that this section concentrates, though the
principles indicated are of general relevance. It is important that
here, too, we should be specially aware of the pitfalls and hazards.

First, one of the most pervasive mistakes is to forget that it is
necessary to compare like with like. It is too easy to slip from one
kind of discourse to another without recognizing the transition, or
to assume that two kinds of discourse are using the same language
about the same thing. For example, the Church can be discussed
both theologically and sociologically. As the pilgrim people of
God the Church understands itself in relation to God as a reality
that exists in history and is therefore incomplete, awaiting an
eschatological fulfilment. The Church's self-understanding thus
carries theological connotations which are asserted independently of the social reality of the Church. Moreover, there is an
ethical dimension to the Church's understanding of itself, which
suggests how the Church ought to behave in its mission to society.
Sociologically, however, the Church is a fragmented, loosely
identified scattered reality, caught up in nationalistic, class and
cultural conflicts. It is hard to know what counts: is it the institutional structures, the devotions and liturgies, or the professed
belief? Theology provides a description of reality as understood
in relation to God, whereas sociology tries to make empirical,
historical sense of a pattern of human behaviour.

Yet it is not enough to say that we have here two parallel
'stories' about the same thing, to which we could add others such
as psychology or anthropology. They both do indeed refer to the
same thing but they both also offer an explanation. The two must
enter into dialogue with one another because they illuminate each
other and contribute to whatever may be the ultimate truth about
the Church. This dialogue may not cease before the end of time,

but it will be a way of enriching our understanding in the meantime! Sociology can show us how religion really works in society and may enlarge or correct our theological understanding. At the same time, the sociologist can recognize that the reality to which theology points does have content and importance for the way sociology views religion. Such a dialogue, however, must be careful and patient, open and mutually critical.

Secondly, such a dialogue, however, is always in danger of becoming unbalanced. One of the partners threatens to usurp the other. Theology is always taking on partners in its search for faith understanding. In modern theology this has classically been with philosophy and history. More recently, hermeneutics and Marxist critical theory have also been employed alongside the other social sciences. The threat, however, is always that the critical tool imposes itself and controls the theological reality.

It has frequently been pointed out that much modern pastoral care has surrendered its theological content to the assumptions of humanistic, Jungian or other psychologies. Perhaps a classic example was Paul Tillich's near equation of justification by faith with aspects of existential psychology. There can in fact be a danger of real incompatibility between the theoretical assumptions of the discipline being drawn on and the Christian tradition. They can be very uneasy bedfellows. Some go even further, as exemplified by this comment from Peter Bellamy when discussing some of the theories used by pastoral counselling borrowed from secular contexts:

> As a basis for counselling in a Christian context, humanistic psychology is unacceptable. It is hostile to fundamental Christian beliefs and practices.[2]

Great discrimination has to be exercised. It may be that certain forms of the social sciences are in greater or lesser harmony with the Christian perspective and thus provide better working partners than others. At other points it may be possible to separate out the tools of social analysis from the accompanying metaphysical theories. This is the claim made by liberation theology in its use of Marxist analysis – a claim still hotly debated. Meanwhile the dialogue goes on.

Third, the opposite tendency is to deny validity to the social science and to make theology the dominant or sole partner.

A good example of this is the so-called biblical counselling of Jay Adams. He claims that the Bible supplies all that is necessary concerning the aims and methods of counselling. He reduces all counselling to morality and repentance. Yet there is an uncanny similarity to the behaviourist therapy of Skinner and, again, instead of dialogue we have monologue. There is, of course, a proper place for theology. As we have suggested, the authority of the tradition, with the Bible at its heart, has a legitimate and crucial part to play; without it practical theology ceases to be Christian. Nevertheless, theological imperialism does not make for a creative conversation with other disciplines.

Dialogue with colleagues

The other expression of the dialogical nature of practical theology is with others with whom we work. This is most strongly exemplified in the relation between the ministry and other caring professions.

Celia is a student on placement from the local theological college. She is not an ordinand but has a commitment to some kind of pastoral activity and has decided to equip herself with a pastoral qualification. Her community work placement is in a large community centre run from an old Victorian Methodist church. The community worker is appointed by the local authority but many of the activities are church related and run by church members. It is a busy and valued place. Once a month the local caring professionals meet for lunch and are joined by the community liaison officers from the local schools and the police, the community health workers and some clergy. All this is exciting and valuable for Celia as it brings her close to the kinds of work she enjoys and those who could be her potential partners.

She is, however, also quickly learning a few things about inter-disciplinary working. The first is the importance of being a recognized professional. The qualification she is taking, however valuable and competent, does not carry much weight since it would not be recognized by anyone outside a limited circle. She will have to get another qualification to be accepted as professionally competent. Indeed, this currently concerns her college which is trying to ensure that her degree scheme carries national professional recognition, so that she has the same qualification as her colleagues in the public sector. Moreover it is clear that the clergy are viewed very oddly. Are they colleagues or are they amateurs? Those who are respected are either the one or two with previous professional expertise or those who are willing to defer to others. But there is also considerable inter-professional rivalry. Each profession has its own culture and expectations. Lines are very carefully drawn. Those outside the charmed circle are regarded with some suspicion. Yet there is also a lot of genuine caring and selfless service, of people trying to do a worthwhile job under very difficult conditions and working with clients who are almost impossibly trying. Celia is full of admiration.

In describing all this back in a college tutorial group session, Celia found that Stewart had another example of inter-professional working to offer. He had been in the local teaching hospital and had had a session with the chaplaincy team. What had fascinated him was an obvious clash between the senior Catholic chaplain and the youngest member of the team, a lay Quaker woman. The Catholic saw his task as being part of the healing team. The hospital, including the chaplaincy, was there for the patients. In the processes of medical care each played a recognizable part: doctor, nurse, social worker, etc. The chaplain cared for the spiritual welfare of his patients. This was his expertise and authority. Each professional should stick to his task. Then everyone knows their place. But the Quaker saw the pastoral task as having a number of complementary dimensions: the healing work with patients; but also the pastoral needs of the staff, medical support and administrative; and yet again the structural needs of the institution itself – its values and tasks, the way people are treated and the pressures of efficiency and solvency. This latter perspective suggested that far from the chaplaincy being simply part of the system it was also there as a stranger alongside and in dialogue with the system. As such it should sit free of any normal professional structure. These reports from Celia and Stewart led the group to discuss the nature and importance of professionalism.

Modern society has witnessed a growing professionalization. Over many decades different groups have sought to secure their identity and worth by claiming professional or craft (union) status. This is an expression of increased technological innovation and specialization. Today it is possible to look up the Yellow Pages and engage a specialist service for almost anything. Despite the attempt in recent years to curtail restrictive practices in the

professions and the unions, the tendency towards professionalization will not go away.

A profession or similar group offers a service on the basis of a
guaranteed training, expertise and code of conduct. This is
safeguarded by stringent entry requirements and an internal peer-
based discipline. There are clear advantages. The client knows what
is being offered has a level of competence. The professional has a
marketable qualification and a collegial structure. So it has seemed
desirable to many to try to gain such a recognition. Thus teachers,
social workers and counsellors have pursued this grail over recent
years, with varying degrees of success.

Clergy, however, are in an anomalous position. They have been
one of the traditional professions, alongside law and medicine.
Over the past two hundred years they have also acquired many of
the modern features of a profession. Thus the minister is regarded
as the religious specialist, offering a particular service, mostly
liturgical, together with some kind of pastoral/spiritual guidance.
But the pattern is not quite complete. Unlike the law and medicine the clergy never became a 'hard' profession. This was due to
a complex series of reasons, not least the changing place of
religion in modern society. Thus the clergy were never, as a body,
a closed shop or a strictly disciplined group.

At the same time, especially in recent decades, there has been a
shift in the perception of religion. Society is now pluralistic and
religion is a matter of choice between competing alternatives.
Secondly, religion is regarded as a private personal activity rather
than part of the public domain. Gradually Christianity and
society have drawn apart. The clergy, too, especially in the established churches, have found themselves less and less publicly
accepted figures and more and more restricted to serving the
church community.

The issue of professionalization

These two factors come together to pose real problems for the
clergy, problems which are brought into focus around the issue of
professionalism.

(i)   One reaction is to assert the professionalization of the min-
      istry. Its competence is theological and pastoral. To take this
      stand will strengthen the tendency to view the ministerial

task as being directed to those who seek the professional services – increasingly those within the practising Christian community. But it is also an option for those who would want to maintain the public dimension of ministry in the secular community. An example of this would be Stewart's Catholic hospital chaplain. The full-time chaplain is paid for by the Health Service to work in the hospital. In such a position the chaplain has to establish his or her credibility. One obvious way is to set the chaplain alongside the other professions and to become part of the healing team with an appropriate competency. This is a model that has recently been strengthened by a Health Service obsessed with appraisals and cost effectiveness. Indeed hospital chaplains, as do forces chaplains, have a strong professional identity with their own organizations.

(ii) A second approach, however, would move in the opposite direction and question the validity of the professional model for clergy. There is no intention of denying the need for high levels of integrity or competence. But it asks whether religion is only one facet of human existence alongside others, or whether it has to do with the whole of life as lived under God. If so the minister cannot be boxed into professional structures but should sit loose to all human institutions, having a prophetic freedom and a primary responsibility to truth and justice. Within the sphere of hospital chaplaincy this is represented by those who see the chaplain as a clown or jester.[3] She or he is part of the organization but something of a maverick within it, free to ask questions, to cut corners, and to build bridges. The court fool is both a favourite and a butt, sitting in the King's counsels yet alone and marginalized. It is not the easiest of roles to play. Another group who work in this way are the industrial chaplains. They are not appointed by industry but negotiate entry. They have no status other than that which they win.

(iii) A third approach to the issue of professionalization is to recognize the importance of representative persons. This brings us back to the point of ministry in the public domain. Both hospital and industrial chaplains are examples of those who put themselves in the world as representatives of the Church. Theirs is primarily an affirmation of the value of Christian faith to the secular community. Yet the pressure is to find areas of work where their expertise is welcome so that they justify their presence in concrete ways. So the hospital chaplain is co-opted onto the ethics committee and the industrial chaplain gets involved in the training courses for apprentices. The search for relevance is always present. For others it can take the form (more in America than here) of offering professional counselling or in becoming involved in educational or other community activity. Some could only resolve the tension between Church and world by taking secular employment as a vehicle of ministry in social work, schools or the Health Service.

These three reactions to ministry in the world today tend to jostle each other uneasily. Few resolve it in an absolute way. The vast majority recognize the inevitable tension between loyalty and service within the community of faith, and the call to witness and serve in the world. In this the pastor is only living out that which every Christian in some sense experiences.

However the dilemma is coped with practically, the minister is always in a situation of collaboration and dialogue. In the traditional village the parson, doctor, school teacher, police officer and nurse are often an informal team, each with their own special tasks but coming together in a shared service of the community. In a more populous and diverse context such as the inner city or council estate, such an alliance has to be deliberately built. Whether formally in regular meetings, or informally through daily personal contact, there can be real inter-professional co-operation and learning.

This is part of the inter-disciplinary task of practical theology. It is why many courses insist on a placement of some kind with a caring agency. It is valuable for learning more of the skills involved in pastoral care. But it is also valuable as a way of getting to know something of another professional culture; to appreciate the legal and professional constraints; to explore the underlying philosophy and attitudes that inform practice; to learn and demystify the jargon; to see how they see others, not least the clergy; and to know what each can expect from the other. It is also important to be aware of what is happening to colleagues in other fields: the threat of redundancy; the effect of new legislation; the pressures of being under-resourced. This is a continuous learning process. Time spent in meetings, on committees, and working together, is not wasted. It is that which creates effective collaboration.

There are, however, constant pressures put on clergy by the caring and other socially related professions. The first is that the churches, together with the clergy, are still one of the most important community groups in an area and they are, by definition, committed to caring and service. This means that when allies are sought it is to the churches that the other professionals turn, especially to the minister as the public representative. It is as though all social concerns must be taken up by what are often very hard-pressed Christian communities. Secondly, there is often an expectation that clergy should be professionally competent in exactly the same fields as the partner professional. Called to the bedside of a dying patient by the community nurse, a minister, even with competent pastoral skills, is not necessarily going to step into the situation with all the confidence of another caring professional. The ministry is very varied and broad in scope and a particular minister may be more competent in other areas outside the requirements of pastoral counselling. Sometimes one gets the feeling that other professionals would say, to parody *My Fair Lady*, 'If only the clergy were more like us!'

However, the Church's primary task is to serve the Kingdom. Both the congregation and the minister serve the world not, in the first place, by conforming to the world's expectations of professional competence, but by being those who serve Christ and give service in the world in his name. It is necessary, therefore, to hold in balance the reasonable demands and expectations of those who want to use the Church as a resource and the proper need for the people of God to express its own distinctive witness as to what constitutes the real hope of the world.

Notes

1   See also Pattison, Stephen, 'The Use of Behavioural Sciences in Pastoral Studies' in Ballard, Paul H., *The Foundations of Pastoral Studies and Practical Theology* (University College, Cardiff 1986), pp. 79–85.
2   In Ballard, op. cit., p. 95.
3   See Faber, Hije, *Pastoral Care in the Modern Hospital* (SCM 1971).

Chapter 9

Theological reflection

It was Tuesday morning. The staff team of St Mary-the-Less straggled in from the Communion service, gathering for their regular meeting. The format was usually the same. It started with Bible study on the Gospel reading for next Sunday, followed by a check through the parish diary for the coming week. They then discussed any matter of wider concern, an issue of policy, or plans for a particular project; then pastoral matters would be shared, information exchanged, and away they would all go to the job. Nearly always in these meetings some valuable discussion took place, opening out into broader theological pastures but still anchored in the practical realities of ministry in that church.

Sometimes the stimulus would come from the biblical passage which was found to throw new light on an issue or problem in church life. On other occasions, the discussion of a church project would be found to resonate with the biblical passage which had been read previously. Or reference would be made to someone's sermon last Sunday and a controversial point made in it. Or someone would comment on the choice of hymns, and the staff would soon enter an exchange of views on a theology of hymnody and modern choruses. The possibilities were endless, and the discussions both interesting in themselves and also of major importance in shaping thinking and practice in church life.

What had been going on was theological reflection. This is the third stage of the pastoral cycle. Having started by looking at the contingencies of the situation we are working on, we then moved into examining and exploring the issues it raises in the light of other relevant disciplines. We now come to the crucial core of the enterprise of practical theology, that of reflecting theologically on the situation in order to see where it fits into the mission of God. There is nothing esoteric about this seemingly elusive activity. It simply holds together the practice of ministry with the resources of theology and allows the interaction to guide what we do next. The staff team of St Mary-the-Less were either starting from 'theology' (next Sunday's Gospel) or from the particularities of ministry (discussion of projects or people). They brought with them their knowledge and experience of other disciplines of thought and action, and their own self-knowledge, and out of the 'critical conversation' between these various elements came the activity we call 'theological reflection'.

The problem with such reflection is not its scarcity but its lack of precision at key moments. Christian people are always thinking theologically, whether in rudimentary or sophisticated ways; their discussions will always betray a theological stance of some sort. The problem is rather that such reflection is all too easily allowed to remain uncritical or unfocused. Clergy forget the rigorous thinking of theological college and slip into unreflective pragmatism. They also forget that one of the key tasks of ordained ministry or church leadership is to facilitate more informed theological debate, so that the Church may be led into all truth (John 16.13). Theological reflection is thus one of the crucial arts of ministry, to be both practised and taught. It is simply the art of making theology connect with life and ministry so that Gospel truth comes alive.

Where theological reflection fits into practical theology

We have identified practical theology as the enterprise which reflects theologically on the action of the Church both in its own life and in the life of society. Its raw materials are the actions of faith rather than the language of faith. It follows that theological reflection is at the heart of the nature and task of practical theology. It is the key moment of theological engagement with the experience or action under review.

We have also seen how praxis approaches to practical theology usually involve some version of the 'pastoral cycle':

- particularity of the pastoral event, be it a painful bereavement visit, a controversial meeting of the school Governors, or the resignation of the community worker;

- exploration, whereby the insights of other disciplines are brought into play to illuminate the background to the particular event;
- reflective moment of the cycle, where an attempt is made to understand the event in terms of the theological tradition;
- action, where the fruits of the cycle are expressed in active form as part of the Church's ongoing mission.

This pastoral cycle is a basic method of learning from experience, informed both by theology and relevant social theory. It contains within itself, at the stage of reflection, the crucial moment when the practitioner has to relate the experience to the theology. He has to put together the depth and complexity of the experience, and insights gained from the Christian heritage of faith, so as to discover God's presence and action in the midst of the contingencies of this situation. This is theological reflection.

Methods of theological reflection

A crucial point to grasp here is that the various methods of theological reflection described below correspond to the models of practical theology set out in Chapter 5 – applied theology, critical correlation, praxis, habitus. Our claim in that chapter, and in Chapter 6, was that the pastoral cycle, characteristic of the praxis approach to practical theology, does in fact offer a unifying methodology to which the best features of the other models may contribute. The cycle of experience–exploration–reflection–action, offers a structure for thinking and a way of acting which take account of the insights of all the approaches to practical theology.

It will be no surprise therefore that at the key moment in practical theology, that of theological reflection, not all the methods used are based on a praxis approach, but many are drawn from other models of practical theology. There is the possibility of great richness of method when it comes to reflection, and the reader will notice how the strengths of various models are used throughout this chapter. We are therefore drawing out the implications of all the main approaches to practical theology outlined in Chapter 5.

As Christians attempt to think theologically about practical issues and events they will use methods which appeal to them for complex theological, temperamental and cultural reasons. A highly analytical approach, using steps of logic and critical appraisal, will not appeal very much to someone who tends to work more on an instinctive, intuitive level. Someone who tells stories and thinks in metaphors is unlikely to be drawn to the discipline of a verbatim account of a pastoral encounter. Cultural factors will also come into play. An African context may mean that indigenous Christians have more of a sense of the numinous and religious, more sense of community and the harmony of peoples, more symbolism and celebration in Christian worship and living.[1] Their theological reflection will echo these features of their faith. A different form of theological reflection is likely to appeal to someone in the West brought up in the post-Enlightenment atmosphere of critical thinking and analytic observation. It is important therefore to be aware of a wide range of possibilities in thinking theologically about practice.

Linear approaches: applied theology

The most basic form of theological reflection is that which operates in a linear mode whereby the Christian asks what biblical material – narrative, teaching, parable, law-code, poetry, prophecy – seems particularly relevant to the situation under review. When a connection has been made, biblical wisdom and authority give the necessary insights into the current issue. Not just the Bible, but other sources of Christian truth may also be used: for example, the teaching of the Church, or models of systematic theology. The authority of a given wisdom applies directly to the situation under consideration.

A church council was discussing its policy on the marriage of people who had been divorced. Jesus' teaching in Scripture seemed uncompromising: a second marriage would be adultery except in cases of unfaithfulness. A minority on the council thought the biblical material was more complex, but the church decided to take the meaning of Scripture at face value, and to try and apply it with maximum compassion and encouragement for those who might be hurt. The policy was not to judge, but to offer Christ's forgiveness, and to have a good, strong service of prayer after the civil marriage.

Another church wanted to embark on a responsible ministry of healing. The vicar called together a core group including a GP and a psychotherapist, and together they planned a strategy. Their first task was to study the Scriptures and survey what biblical authority undergirded a contemporary ministry of healing. Thus satisfied, a sermon course was set up to involve the congregation, and a weekend conference with the Archbishops' Adviser on the ministry of healing. When the biblical warrant was clear, and the appropriate health practitioners had been consulted, the work proceeded.

The strengths of such an approach are attractive. The method is clear and rooted in hundreds of years of scriptural or ecclesial authority. It cuts through the potential evasions and compromises of a Church which may want to make a premature peace with a changing culture. It applies the consistent norms of a revealed faith to the relativism of contemporary moral debate.

Nevertheless this approach may assume a too simple relationship between tradition and practice. It may ignore not only God's continuing self-revelation in history but also the possibility that he might be creatively at work in other disciplines such as psychology or the social sciences and that truth might be found there also. It is in danger of making a hermeneutical leap from the biblical 'horizon' to the current situation without taking sufficiently seriously the complexity of other descriptions of the contemporary social order. In an extreme form this approach may even implicitly locate God in a book, a church or a lecture room and disregard the conviction of faith that God will be found already at work in the ambiguities and struggles of the modern world.

Correlational methods

While the linear approach to theological reflection may be a straightforward method with a long pedigree, correlational approaches have become common in more recent theological discussion. As we outlined in Chapter 5, Paul Tillich in the 1960s led the way into correlation, offering theology a way of speaking to modern debates by identifying contemporary human needs and preoccupations and then finding the theology which could interact with the language used in those debates.[2] The conversation partner Tillich used most often was that of so-called 'depth psychology' and that now has a rather dated feel to it. However, the approach has been refined by Tracy and other writers in the field of practical theology so that a 'revised correlational method' has emerged which puts into a critical conversation the distinctive elements of the situation under review, the human science or other material which throws light on it, and the theology which bears most directly.[3] Out of this discussion emerges the understanding, which then leads to action.

Case studies

One effective correlational method of theological reflection is that of the disciplined case study. In some forms, this approach can almost be a microcosm of the pastoral cycle, revealing a considerable overlap between praxis and correlation at this point.

A group of students were presented, before their seminar, with a two-page account of a significant event in the life experience of one of them. It told of an encounter with a man who was homeless and psychologically disturbed. The case study was written in the form of a brief description of the events, an analysis of social and psychological factors involved, appropriate theological themes and an evaluation of his action in this situation. The student had ten minutes to answer questions of fact and then remained silent while the rest of the group engaged in discussion, bringing up ideas, responses, theology and critique. Theological discussion centred around issues of community and responsibility. They considered the case of the demon-possessed man in Mark 5, and the structural sin which society often tolerates almost unconsciously. They talked about the limits of charity and what it meant to be made in the image of God. At the end of an hour, the student gave his response to the discussion, evaluating the ideas which had emerged and indicating what he might have done differently another time.

The value of this particular approach is that it enables a degree of rigour to be applied both by the student and by his peers. The clear disciplined progression means that no stage of the process is rushed, and honest discussion and critique are encouraged. The silence of the student, though difficult, is important as it prevents a question-and-answer approach, or a form of self-justification, but rather allows an open reflective process to develop from which all may learn.

The case study method is of course one which involves a degree of artificiality in the slowing up of reflection almost to snail's pace! However, the value of this method of reflection becomes obvious when it is used, and it may remain in the student's or practitioner's mind as one particular example of an important general practice in ministry. In initial and continuing theological training the process is of considerable value, and if a staff team in a church can bring itself to take it seriously as an occasional practice, the benefits would usually be clear. Above all it impresses on the student and minister the importance of thinking theologically about ministry and mission rather than acting from habit or prejudice.

The spidergram

This approach is a written form of brainstorming. It draws on the ability of the mind to make connections of a lateral as well as a linear nature, opening up the possibility of people seeing links they had not initially imagined or realized could be there. It is a good method of opening up a debate or blowing fresh material into the reflection.

The group had spent a week making contact with various agencies working in the field of race relations. They had a great store of raw material, including stories they had heard, impressions they had gained, theological themes which were beginning to play around the mind. In order to start the reflective process and begin to see some links, the group was split into sub-groups with large pieces of paper and felt-tip pens. Their task was first to identify a key theological concept which seemed to them to be central to the week's experiences: these ranged from 'the Kingdom of God' to 'the person of Jesus Christ'. From that central concern written in the middle of the piece of paper, they then started drawing out a spider's web of issues – fragments of conversation, biblical stories, social and historical factors and more. They then set about connecting ideas with lines and circles to try to see some shape in all this material, and what theology was appropriate. When all the groups came together and shared their insights the discussion became mutually enlightening and surprising, as new depths were discovered in the common experience they had all been through.

There is value in this approach not only in group reflection but also in personal supervision or even solo work. The objectivity and visual impact of a piece of paper allow the reflection to take on a clarity and shape which is not always present in 'the slimy mud of words, the sleet and hail of verbal imprecisions'.[4] It takes the richness of a situation seriously and is open to the contribution of any information or insight from another relevant discipline.

However, the issue to be faced with any correlational approach to theological reflection is that it may lack criteria for giving adequate relative weighting to different sources of information in the conversation. Presuming that the Bible or tradition has a normative status for the Christian, how is that to be evaluated? Here we are up against the hermeneutical problem of how to handle the text responsibly. The Bible was written by many people over many years in a culture distant from our own. How do we interpret such a strange series of documents? We hear the Word of God spoken to and through the Church throughout time, but what are the limits to interpretation? How do we evaluate the testimony of the text when other claims to truth and wisdom from psychology, social anthropology, history, literature and other disciplines seem to press in different directions, affirming different truths?

How much weight, for example, is to be given to what the Bible says about homosexuality and how much to the plethora of confusing insights from scientific and cultural studies? To reject all that science and anthropology say on the subject because of the teaching of Leviticus and Romans would be folly; to accept the pronouncements of the latest scientific study would be equally unwise and put theological reflection at the mercy of scientific debate. These are some of the problems which are raised by a correlational approach to theological reflection.

Praxis approaches

It will be seen by now how these different approaches to theological reflection mirror the main models of practical theology. So far we have encountered linear and correlational models and now we face praxis as a framework. This parallelism is to be expected, of course, because theological reflection is at the heart of practical theology, the key theological moment of the enterprise. As we saw in previous chapters, however, practical theology is more than theological reflection; it is both a set of disciplines and a method of taking the life and action of the Church with theological seriousness. Nevertheless the relationship between practical theology and theological reflection is close, perhaps akin to that between parent and child; the one is echoed in the other. Practical theology is the parent whose best (and worst!) characteristics are seen in theological reflection; on the one hand there is the ability to

make theology come alive, and on the other there is the tendency
to frustrating imprecision.

Praxis approaches to reflection are therefore those which
borrow from the liberation perspectives of local and political
theologies, and in particular, the pastoral cycle. Typically they
hold together human experience and biblical theology in a
structured cycle of learning.

Bible workshop

When John Davies was Principal of the College of the Ascension
in Birmingham he developed a method of enabling all sorts of
Christians to handle the Bible with a modest confidence as they
tackled their life and experience from a faith perspective.[5] The
Bible workshop is a way of holding together a biblical text and the
contingencies of people's lives in a process of mutual illumina-
tion.

Davies calls us 'second Christians' since we have different
questions from the 'first Christians'; for example, our problems
do not centre around the complaints of Jewish Temple officials
concerning the keeping of the Jewish Law, as did the problems of
the early disciples. The men and women who contributed to the
writing of what we know as the New Testament were also 'second
Christians' on this understanding. They were dealing with issues
thrown up by the success of their evangelism and the vivid experiences people were having of the Holy Spirit. They faced questions
about leadership, church discipline and Christian slaves. We, as
they, therefore, have to reflect on our own experience, link it with
the stories of Jesus, and derive mandates for new action in our
contemporary world.

St Swithin's church was experiencing change and it was
causing anxiety. They were considering moving to a 'care in the
community' model of ministry to those in need – an open doors
policy using the church plant as a resource for a whole variety of
community groups. The Bible passage for the home groups was
therefore chosen to help people reflect on this: Mark 5.1–20, the
Gadarene Swine. First, they read the **story** slowly and quietly,
trying to enter it. Then they were asked what **'snaps'** in their
experience they could see immediately, what first impressions,
snapshots, snap connections there were between this incident and
their fears, confusions and anger. This should not yet be a thought
out and theological response, just immediate and instinctive

reactions. Then they embarked on **study**, a serious attempt to grapple with the text in its own setting, using commentaries and maps. Then the group searched for the '**spin-offs**' from the work done so far, focusing on questions like: 'How do we diagnose what is wrong in the church, given the difficulty of diagnosing who or what was in the wrong in Gadara?' 'What is the real cost of healing in the church, and who pays it, given the different perceptions we now have of how many people were in fact "outcasts" in Gadara?' These spin-offs now led into decisions about what to do in the present situation – new 'gospel events'.

A variety of skills is needed in this approach: selection of the right passage, without being manipulative; a leader who could work through the process in a disciplined way; appropriate resources which are not focused on some 'expert' telling the group what is 'right'. Nevertheless the method is straightforward and very rewarding if followed sensibly.

Another 'Bible workshop' approach would be this: a group is trying to handle a potential split in the church between those who emphasize the active social responsibility of Christ's people and those who emphasize the life of prayerful dependence on God. The passage chosen is Luke 10.38–42 about Mary and Martha. The group hears the story vividly told and then divides into three groups representing Mary, Martha and the disciples. The story is then read again and the groups are given the task of discussing, in the first person, how it might feel to be their particular person, and what things they might want to say to the others. The opportunity is then given for open conversation between the three groups of participants, in which the deeply felt issues should emerge with force and clarity. After coming out of role, the group as a whole can then begin to understand the issues faced by the church with greater emotional and intellectual engagement, and can decide on appropriate action to heal the division.

A wide variety of approaches to participatory Bible study have been developed and published in recent years. Care has to be taken that the novelty of the study does not open the door to inadequate hermeneutical method. For instance, the interpreter should not draw over-simple parallels between contemporary dilemmas and biblical stories without first understanding what the story meant when it was first included in the canon of Scripture. Similarly, the interpreter should avoid reducing every modern issue to a different angle on the Prodigal Son!

Nevertheless, the power and attraction of participatory Bible study is beyond doubt.[6]

Liberation methods

A host of methods of theological reflection of greater or lesser complexity have emerged from the perspectives of liberation theology. Juan Luis Segundo employs a hermeneutical circle which begins with a specific situation, from which current questions arise; these questions are put to the traditional content of revelation which, thus interrogated, provides a response which illuminates the individual and social situation.[7] Stephen Pattison, in his *Pastoral Care and Liberation Theology*,[8] lays particular emphasis on social and political analysis using 'tools of suspicion' on the pastoral situation and on the theology and practice of pastoral care. In other words, Christians must beware of making comfortable pastoral judgements about situations without taking seriously the sharp and possibly alien insights of social and political analysts. These liberation methods are thorough but not easily performed 'on the hoof'; they require a serious commitment of time and effort to yield their undoubted benefits.

Popular praxis

A whole variety of different methods exists which lack the theological and analytical rigour of other praxis approaches but make up for that in accessibility.

1. Members of a church group are asked to express their understanding of church life in terms of a shield divided into four quarters. In one quarter they are to depict the church's successes, in another its failures, in another its aspirations, and in the last the biblical character most like it in nature. Underneath they are to inscribe the motto by which the church lives. Out of this exercise comes analysis of the church's character in terms both of social reality and theological identity. This leads to a renewed vision of the purposes of the church at this moment and in this place.

2. Alternatively the above exercise can be undertaken using advertising slogans rather than shields. Each person or group is asked to devise a slogan or an advert for a newspaper which expresses what the church is about and what it offers. How is the church promoting itself? With what emphases? For whose benefit? To the exclusion of whom? The slogans lead into these and other

questions, which are both social and theological in character, and out of which new resolutions may be made

3. A further method of 'popular praxis' is the physical model-ling of the situation as it is seen by those people involved in the reflection. If, for example, a group of students has been on a placement in a large church, the tutor may ask them to work out how they would represent the relationship of the leadership team to the rest of the church, and to do that by using themselves as a 'living sculpture'. As they work out what configurations, poses, distances and interactions to embody in that sculpture, so they will be reflecting on the issues they have encountered in the place-ment and their interpretation. The creation of the sculpture is followed by more detailed discussion which draws on the vivid experience which the modelling will have provided.

Narrative approaches

One of the newer methods of theological reflection, which is also as old as humanity's religious quest itself, is that of narrative. The method essentially belongs to the praxis approach to practical theology inasmuch as it proceeds from experience through analy-sis to action, but it deserves consideration on its own account. By using the fundamental human category of story, which is the primary language of human experience, the process of reflection is able to tap into some of the richest sources of insight we have available. Verbal human interactions are characteristically in narrative form, whether it be friends meeting to catch up on news, or students who are being inducted into the framework of a particular college culture, or children discovering their own family culture at home. Newspapers convey information in stories, as do television programmes, not only in the soap operas which consistently top the ratings, but also in the mini-narratives of advertisements. All cultures are formed and sustained by their narratives, and therefore the story form of theological reflection is clearly based on a deeply rooted narrative approach to under-standing experience.

Telling the story

The tutor sat down with the student who had been on placement and put the first question: 'So tell me what happened, and what you thought was going on.' The student began to tell the story of the placement, which had been hard and confrontational. As he told it, so his interpretations also came out. The origin of the conflict lay in different understandings of ministry and in a fear of failure on the part of the student. This had led to his diffidence and awkwardness. Occasionally the tutor would stop the flow and ask the student to reflect a little further on some phrase he had used, why he had used it, and what the implications were of that understanding of the event. At the end of the narrative the tutor pulled together the main themes of personal and theological interpretation which he had heard, and developed the discussion around those key ideas. What the student had been doing was constructing his own theological critique of the placement, by turning the chronicle into a story, and giving his own interpretations of the significant events.

The strength of this method of reflecting is that it uses the flow of human experience as the vehicle for making sense of it. It builds on the narrative structure of human consciousness.[9] The weakness is that it allows a range of theological responses which are potentially over-subjective. The critical distance has to be provided by the supervisor listening, and she has to be prepared not to collude with the strong investment which the student might have in the validity of his interpretation.

Another of the possibilities of a narrative approach to reflection is that it can be undertaken corporately with the narrative being told by the group. The leader of a parish mission was meeting members of the church to prepare some of the ground. He put up a long piece of wide paper on the wall and marked it off with every decade since the war. He asked the group to remember any year on which a special event took place in the life of the nation or of the world. As they spoke up he wrote them on the chart: 1963, assassination of President Kennedy; 1979, Mrs Thatcher becomes Prime Minister; 1969, first men on the moon; 1989, communism collapses in Eastern Europe; 2003, England win the rugby World Cup, and 2005 the Ashes. The chart soon filled up. Some people were amazed at how inaccurate their memory was; others were surprised at precisely what they did manage to remember. After a while the leader asked the group to do something different. In pairs, would they try to remember what had happened in the life of their parish in that same period? Who had done what, when? What problems and crises had they faced? What major changes in parish policy had there been, new buildings, change of services, stewardship campaigns? After a sluggish start, the room was soon buzzing with memories and laughter. The leader started to mark the wall chart again, parallel to the national events. Eventually the leader stopped the flow. 'That', he said, 'is part of your parish story. It's the story of your mission through the years. All we can do as a mission team is come and help you take your story on, one step further.' The next stage was to ask the group to identify what they thought God was saying and doing with the parish through its story; how did they understand God and his purposes for them in that community; what was 'good news' for that parish?

This form of reflection is a lengthy one but it enables people to be carried along who would be anxious about being told they were going to be involved in a process of theological reflection. It starts with the core material of God's dealings with a human community and develops into full theological thinking by the people of God about their understanding of him and his action with them.

The verbatim report
This method has already been referred to in Chapter 7 in the context of how experience and information are gathered and recorded. We now see how it functions as a method of theological reflection. It is an approach much used in Clinical Pastoral Education in pastoral and social work training. It involves a student writing up a full account of a pastoral encounter soon after the event in such a way that subsequent analysis with a supervisor will reveal the inner processes of the encounter, the strategies being used by both student and 'client', the reasons for success or failure in such strategies, and what is to be learned for the future. This method may or may not be specifically theological in intention, depending on the analytical framework of the supervisor and the questions she asks of the student. She may, however, take the analysis in a clear theological direction by asking what implicit theology was operational in the encounter, what Christian resources the student was aware of and did or did not employ, and other such questions. For a fuller account of how the verbatim works, see Foskett and Lyall's *Helping the Helpers*.

The strength of this approach is its realism, in that the encounter is revealed in as much accuracy as memory allows, making possible an honest appraisal of the approach being taken by the student. The weakness lies precisely in the fallibility of memory and the inherent tendency of the mind to make a story out of a bare chronicle; that is, to rewrite the encounter in terms of how the presenter now makes sense of it, rather than as it actually happened.

Situation reports

As we outlined in Chapter 7 there is a range of learning tools much used in theological reflection, all of which work in a broadly narrative form. Chief among these are the significant event/critical incident report and the pastoral focus. These invite the practitioner or student to go through the situation in a written presentation, drawing inferences of a theological, social and psychological nature from it. As such, these tools are correlational as well as narrative in form; an example can be found in Appendix C.

The artistic method of theological reflection

This approach to reflection is again one which does not fit tidily into the fourfold classification of practical theology in Chapter 5. It lies somewhere between praxis and habitus in its underlying structure, and so it appears here as an important alternative to some of the more cerebral methods we are describing.

Western theological traditions are well anchored in verbal analysis and conceptual thought. There is, however, a parallel tradition which has long been present but which is not usually graced with the description 'theological'. This is the approach of the affective heart rather than the cognitive mind; it is the approach of the arts, the contribution of what is sometimes referred to as the right-hand side of the brain, wherein lie our intuition, imagination and creativity. This theology of the heart has never been lost from the tradition of the Eastern Church, but it needs more consciously recapturing in the West, where it has been somewhat marginalized. One way for the artistic dimension to come back into the theological life of the Church is through encouraging its use in the process of theological reflection on experience.

The occasion was a Bible study with lay Christians on the book of the prophet Zephaniah. The great condemnations of chapter 2, whereby cities and tribes are promised the wrath of God for their faithlessness, were translated into the towns and districts of the region in which the group lived. The charges of the prophet thus became more vivid and personal, and the group spent some time reflecting on the appropriateness of the prophet's message for their time and place. The main response they were asked to make, however, was through the medium of paint, clay and collage. The task was simply to express their reactions to the passage and its application, in these creative forms. The group began thought-fully, trying to get inside the story and the medium, so that the one could reflect the impact of the other. Bold paintings of dark and bright began to emerge; unexpected shapes arose out of the clay; strange juxtapositions of picture and form evolved on large pieces of paper. By the end of the evening the participants were emotionally tired but well satisfied. They felt they had penetrated the message of this obscure prophet in a way they had never expected. By means of the arts they had been reflecting theologically on the complex interplay of Word and world.

The task of having to produce a tangible response to a life expe-rience gives an invaluable focus to Christian thinking. When that response has to be in artistic form the opportunities for distinctive learning are given even greater impetus. It forces the participant to work in new ways and therefore to be at the same time clearer in what she wants to say and also more opaque in allowing the art form to have its own communicative power. Art has a unique ability to 'tell it slant'[10] rather than to make a full frontal, take-it-or-leave-it presentation. Artistic methods therefore allow people to enter into theological reflection with their own experiences and metaphors, the Holy Spirit being the interpreter. This is, of course, also true of other people's art. A group can work with the poetry, music, painting, photograph or sculpture which has come from other people, and then adapt, display or utilize it so that they are able to make their own reflective comments.

A group were presented with dozens of representations of Jesus drawn from different ages and cultures, and from art, sculpture and film. They were asked the question: 'Who is Jesus Christ for you today?' and invited to choose one or two pictures which answered that question for them. In groups, they were then asked to discuss the reasons for their choice and to answer another question: 'What does your choice say about your understanding of mission?' The visual arts have a great potential for facilitating reflection by a different route from the normal cerebral approach.

What is true of the visual arts is also true of other forms of artistic expression. Dance, drama, poetry, creative writing, music – all have the potential to enable people to make a theological response to experience. The possibility is always present that by being so personal such reflection can become self-indulgent and lack any kind of critical distance. Therein lies both the promise and the problem of this method.

The habitus approach

As we outlined in Chapter 5, we are borrowing here from Edward Farley's terminology of habitus as the original goal of the Church's theology.[11] Before any division of theology into spiritual formation and academic study, or still later into a whole range of academic sub-disciplines, the single purpose of theological study was the proper growth of holiness in heart and life. Theology was intended to produce a godly life. In its clarity of vision and its ability to integrate the theological task of the Church, this approach has much to commend it today, as our previous discussion has suggested.

What concerns us here is the particular ways this method may be employed in the crucial task of theological reflection. How can a student, lay person or reflective practitioner bring her whole Christian being to bear on the action or experience she has chosen to review? How can she integrate her thinking, prayer and behaviour in the act of theological reflection in order to take forward the mission of God in this time and place?

Conversation
The art of godly conversation is one form of reflection which combines some of the characteristics of supervision, spiritual direction and a good chat with a Christian friend. A series of simple questions is often all that is necessary to stimulate profound personal reflection on some event or encounter. 'What did you think was really going on there?' 'Where did God seem to be present in that mess?' 'How is all that likely to feed into your prayers?' 'How would you finish the sentence: "From my experience here I have learned that . . ."?' What the supervisor is helping the learner to do is to make some kind of total response to the situation, to re-value the incident in the light of his own Christian character. The method is simple, and simply profound.

'What would Jesus have done?'

This is one of the most straightforward and yet foolhardy approaches to theological reflection. In a sense it is a theologically illiterate question to ask! It seems to by-pass centuries of critical biblical scholarship and hermeneutical theory; it breaks all the rules. Yet the question does continue to have a unique power in helping people to come to the heart of the matter, and to their own heart, in responding to the situation as whole Christian persons, whatever their state of theological sophistication. The discussion can subsequently raise as many issues of interpretation, cultural distance and critical scholarship as the participants want, but the central question remains a challenge to every recipient of it: what is the Christ-like response to this situation?

Liturgy

If liturgy is the technicolour film of theology, one may legitimately expect a liturgical context to provide one of the richest and most comprehensive forms of theological reflection.

It was the end of a weekend course with theological students on the theme of 'Working Together'. The experiences had been diverse and sometimes stretching as they had considered the dynamics of working together in groups, in staff teams, in educational design and in other ways. Working together in sharing the personal treasure of their own spiritual journeys had touched some deep places. The task now was to take all this into worship, applying mind, heart and soul to the reflection, which would be offered to God. They determined their own medium of expression: music, creative writing, the visual arts, a slide/tape meditation, intercessions, drama, dance. The building was filled with a hum of purposeful activity, and soon the elements of the worship began to emerge: poems and songs, freshly minted drama, beautiful artefacts around the altar, heart-breakingly moving slides and music. The reflective process had gone on in the discussion about which readings from the day's papers illuminated the biblical passages and about how to pray with integrity in a situation of conflict. The reflection was also in the hearts and minds of individuals, wrestling with recalcitrant clay and slippery words; and it was in the soul of each person facing that solemn transaction with bread and wine which lies at the heart of every communion service. This was reflection as habitus, the whole group responding to the whole situation with the whole of themselves.

Theological reflection as a tool of ministry

The methods outlined above are simply examples of a process of reflection which lies at the heart of all thoughtful and informed ministry. Many more methods could be adduced; the limitation is mainly that of the imagination. One point ought to be borne in mind, however: theological reflection is characteristically a corporate activity. It is the meeting of minds in common dependence on the tradition and enlivened by the Spirit in searching truth, which yields the insights. A larger group provides the checks and challenges, the insights and lateral thinking, the unexpected questions and the realism necessary to resist the temptations of fantasy. With this important safeguard it can be said with confidence that theological reflection on practice is one of the indispensable tools of ministry. With it we will learn from experience and grow in ministerial maturity. Without it we run the risk either of pastoral ineffectiveness or of great error.

Notes

1   As an example see the radical rethinking of theological method by Vincent Donovan as a missionary priest in Africa: Donovan, V., *Christianity Rediscovered* (SCM Press 1978).

2   Tillich, P., *Systematic Theology* (Chicago University Press 1953).

3   Many practical theologians use a version of the revised correlational method, but see especially: Tracy, D., *The Analogical Imagination* (Crossroad Books 1981).

4   Eliot, T.S., Chorus IX from 'The Rock', *Collected Poems 1909–1962* (Faber and Faber 1963).

5   See the results of his work in Davies, J. and Vincent, J., *Mark at Work* (BRF 1986).

6   A particularly powerful exponent is Weber, H-R., *Transforming Bible Study* (WCC 1981).

7   Segundo, J.L., *The Liberation of Theology* (Gill and Macmillan 1977).

8   Pattison, S., *Pastoral Care and Liberation Theology* (CUP 1994).

9   This understanding of the basic structure of human consciousness is well argued in Crites, S., 'The Narrative Quality of Experience' (*Journal of the American Academy of Religion*, vol. 39, 1971) pp. 291–311.

10   The phrase is from Emily Dickinson.

11   See particularly: Farley, E., *Theologia* (Fortress Press 1983), in which he traces the historical development of the concept of habitus. Sam Wells also develops the argument for a 'habitus' approach to Christian ethics in his *Improvisation: The drama of Christian ethics* (SPCK 2004) where he states, 'It becomes clearer that the great majority of things the Christians do derive from habit and instinct, and that Christian ethics is more concerned with the development of good habits than with the making of good decisions' (p. 152).

Chapter 10

Mission in context today

So far, in Part II, we have been following the dynamic of the pastoral circle, moving from present experience through enquiry and analysis to theological reflection. It will go on to action (Chapter 11). Here, however, it may be as well to pause and stay with the theme of theological reflection but from a somewhat different angle. The intention is to look at three themes which have already been mentioned from time to time and to bring them together.

The first is the recent and growing interest in congregational studies. These stress that each congregation has its own characteristics and behavioural patterns. Such characteristics express its fundamental perspectives and beliefs that have come out of its experience and story. As a Christian community these will reveal the often unspoken, hidden convictions about God and the world, Jesus and salvation. In other words there is a corporate 'habitus'. So there is a need to understand and to work on the corporate aspects of theological reflection.

Second, especially in the great conurbations, British society has become increasingly pluralistic. Most obviously this has been the result of increased immigration, part of a world trend, that has brought ethnic, cultural and religious diversity into many communities. But that is merely one visible expression of a widespread change across the whole of society. This fragmented society has been called post-modern, though there is considerable debate as to what this may mean and how it will work out.

Third, not least in reaction to that social change, the Church has had to reassess its situation. What is its place in a pluralistic society? How should it understand its ministry and mission?

Looking at a congregation

This is where we catch up with Barbara who has recently moved to a new charge at St Thomas' Uniting Church, a small local ecumenical project (LEP – Methodist/URC) in Ivytown, an older residential district of Wanderdon, a fairly large industrial town. She recognizes that this is a very different world both from her recent rural pastorate and her suburban childhood. This is the world of the inner-city and urban living.

Ivytown is not untypical. It is just across the inner ring road that encircles the old settlement of Wanderdon and which is now its 'central business district' and old, decaying industrial core. Ivytown has its own small industrial estate down by the former rail yards. That end is working class, with rows of late nineteenth-century terraced houses. On the other side of the small shopping centre that straddles the main bus route through the area are the old terraced middle-class villas. Up the hill are some roads of larger detached houses, mostly subdivided or replaced by blocks of flats. There is also a small inter-war council estate which is now mostly privately owned.

The shops form the focus of the district. There are still signs of the older working class and 'white collar' families, though they are now mostly elderly. They are catered for by the two traditional pubs, one of which still reveals its Irish origins of the nineteenth-century immigration, as does the Catholic church. There are still a few traditional shops – butcher, baker, and an ironmonger; but most of the other shops are run by Asian families and reflect the new immigrant culture. There are people using this busy street not only from the Indian subcontinent but also from the Middle East, often revealing their origins by wearing traditional dress. There are two mosques, reflecting the ethnic and faith diversity of the new community. One of them is in the grounds of the old grammar school which has been refurbished to form a Muslim faith school. The other school in the area is a state primary school, itself ethnically diverse. The secondary school is just across the railway lines in the next district. There is also an African population, some Afro-Caribbean but also a number from West Africa, whose women dress resplendently for special occasions, which includes going to church. The old Presbyterian chapel, which was the old United Reformed Church (URC), now part of the LEP, is now a lively black-led Pentecostal church. There is also a growing, mainly white, independent evangelical congregation, now seeking premises. St George's, the parish church, sits in its own square just behind the shops. Interestingly, it hosts a small Indian congregation. The Sikh gurdwara is on the edge of Ivytown, on the ring road, but that means that there is a significant Sikh presence. Surprisingly, perhaps, among the Tandoori and Balti restaurants there are a couple of wine bars, a bookstore and a boutique. This, as do also some of the cars, including the occasional 4 × 4 Chelsea tractor, parked outside, signifies an influx of young professionals seeking desirable but cheaper accommodation. This may also account for the centre for meditation and alternative therapies next to the library.

On her first Sunday morning, despite the preparatory visits, Barbara wondered what she would find. There were some forty or fifty people waiting to greet her. The majority were elderly, with a preponderance of women, though there were some families, including a single mum, from the older communities. There were also some young professionals, mostly with children. These two groups provided the core of the Junior Church. Scattered across the church were an Asian and two Afro-Caribbean couples. It was a warm, caring community which, while pretty traditional liturgically, was concerned and expectant.

Barbara spent the first year settling in and finding her way around, not least the neighbourhood and the city. She learnt that the formative moment for the congregation was when the two churches had joined. Both had been fairly staid lower-middle-class nonconformist chapels, but they had shared a minister prior to the amalgamation which had happened five years before. He had been fairly dynamic and his pragmatic personality had forced them to ask practical questions. They were enthused by the possibility of rationalizing the situation. It was also his vision that suggested that when the single congregation was formed, opportunity should be taken to rebuild and include a community centre. This had been followed by finding funding for a full-time community worker, Jim.

So the place was busy. Alongside the traditional churchy activities – Bible study, women's meeting, children's groups – there was a large range of other organizations addressing some of the needs of the community – pre-school groups, latch-key and homework clubs, pensioners groups, English as second language, disability support groups; some set up by Jim and his band of volunteers, others run by outside bodies.

All in all, St Thomas' seemed to have a positive and active presence in the neighbourhood. But there was one anxiety. While she was very happy with both the congregation and the centre, Barbara felt that the church had not really thought through its theological self-understanding. Ivytown had changed and was continuing to change rapidly. There had been no reflection on what this might mean for a Christian community. They were working out of older traditions without having drawn them together or asking whether they were still adequate.

Indeed, as she listened, discovering the strengths and weaknesses of the situation, both within and beyond the people who frequented the church centre, there was cause for a little cautionary concern. Two things became apparent. First, within the different communities on her patch there were many and diverse opinions as to where the neighbourhood was and ought to be going. There was considerable suspicion and defensiveness on all sides. Rapid social change causes anxiety, exacerbated here by the need for many to adjust to a strange new environment, often without the linguistic or practical skills. But there was also a great deal of hope, even if there was little agreement as to how to handle multiculturalism. A great deal of time and effort was being expended by some from every group to develop good neighbourliness. Ivytown was far from being a powder keg; but who could tell what might happen if some fanatics started playing on the suspicions and discontents? It needed patience and goodwill on all sides. Meanwhile, most people went about their daily tasks in their own circles, acknowledging but hardly rubbing shoulders with those from other groups.

Second, Barbara recognized that the people in and attached to the congregation were very much part of the situation: a cross-section of the wider community. But as a company of those who sought to serve Christ, they (with the other congregations) were also committed to see themselves and Ivytown through the eyes of the gospel. Of course this had already begun, albeit unrecognized and unformulated. They worshipped, celebrated the sacraments, read the Bible. Barbara found a good deal of Christian wisdom, sometimes from surprising quarters. And not unexpectedly, people were at different points on the road trying to match their personal experience and anxieties to faith in Christ. As a result, as already suggested, there was little common understanding of St Thomas' ministry and mission. So for her second year, Barbara proposed that time be taken to look at their understanding of their commitment as a congregation. She suggested a series of mini-conferences, with the themes being taken up at the same time in the preaching and Bible study.

As she thought about it and took advice, the issue that kept returning was the nature and impact of pluralism and the situation in Ivytown. Three distinct and yet inter-linked themes emerged as a way of approaching the primary question.

(i)   As a church deeply involved in community work, what is the relation of that to the gospel?
(ii) Living in a multi-cultural community, how do people of different faiths live creatively together?
(iii) What is the true nature of mission for a Christian community that wants to live by and share its faith in such a context?

Witness and service

It felt reasonable and natural to start where the people of St Thomas' were and to look at their community programme first. Why should the church get involved with community work? How was this to be understood in relation to the rest of the church's life?

There were, of course, several answers. A few suggested that it was a way of showing that the Church cared and was a way of witnessing to their faith. In other words, community work was a kind of 'pre-evangelism'. While all agreed that it was important for faith to show itself in 'good works' (James 2.17) most felt that this, as it stood, was over-simplistic. The link between witness and service needed further teasing out. There was also the possibility, if this was the sole motive, of being manipulative, using it simply as a means to another end. Was it true that community activities were only there to point to something else? If so, was there not the danger of them hiding the real agenda and for people to feel that they were being 'softened up', that the real intention was to create Christians? Naturally there was always the hope that people would be attracted into the fellowship, and indeed some had so been drawn in. But it was equally important to relate to people for their own sake, as people, with nothing other than a concern for their well-being and that of the community around.

So others argued that community service was there simply to meet people's needs and to contribute to the well-being of the neighbourhood. But if that were all, some queried, good and proper as it was, what is the difference between that and any other social work? Is that not the job of the statutory services? It suggests that the church is only a voluntary community with no distinct perspective. There were many other voluntary agencies. What, therefore, is the church's specific contribution to the community? To enlarge on this point there were those who wanted to claim that helping to build community and to enable people to improve their lives is itself a gospel sign, a mark of the Kingdom, even though the Name is not named. True, responded others, the Spirit is at work in all places and at all times and there are occasions when this is more or less discernible. But is it not also the Church's task to tell it as it is and to name the Name? It is not that the Church is God's only or even main instrument, but it is the body of those who witness to God's activity in Christ through the Spirit. Not to be known as those who follow Christ is to deny the very foundation of the Church's existence.

At this point Jim intervened. He pointed out that what the church had committed itself to was 'community development'. Community development had its own principles: that is of working *with* people and not simply *for* people. Working *for* people is community service, providing a service in response to a perceived need. Such an approach does properly contribute much to the welfare of a community. There are situations where the only intervention possible is to come to people's aid. The churches have been good at this and it is one of the pillars of the Welfare State. The drawback can be that control is in the hands of the provider, which can leave the recipients in a position of dependency and for the agenda to be dictated from the outside. By working *with* people the emphasis is on collaboration, involvement and self-help. It is about enabling people increasingly to take charge over their own lives and to develop their own strengths and skills. The reason why such an attitude is to be preferred, Jim suggested, is that it is in line with Jesus' ministry of building relationships and offering liberation and a new life. Jesus never forces people but addresses them where they are and values them for their own sakes. However much we want to draw others into the community of faith, we are there *with* them, seeking the common good and the welfare of the wider community.

All these considerations, when taken together, seemed to end up in a paradox. The Christian community is pulled in two ways: to witness to the gospel and to call people to faith, and to be there to serve and to be *with* people in and for the sake of the community around, however little and piecemeal that may be. But, on reflection, this is not an either–or situation. They realized that the boundaries were not so clear cut. All the members of the congregation, including Barbara and Jim, were also part of the wider community as members of families, neighbours and in their jobs. They lived in this ambiguity of being visibly Christians and yet ordinary members of their various groupings where properly and naturally those considerations came first. Conversely, people from the neighbourhood came in and out of the building and ran its organizations for all manner of reasons, and not a few were members of other faith communities or avowedly disclaimed any faith allegiance. Yet these, too, were part of the fabric of St Thomas' community. Often it was a kind of home from home, a place that was good to be in and to be associated with. They shared many of the hopes and vision of the congregation for each other and those around with whom they also shared in the activities. There was much common ground despite real differences.

Out of these discussions an analogy was suggested that expressed the emerging vision of the church's self-understanding. This was that of a wheel, of which Christ is the hub, the central point from which the spokes radiate. He it is that holds all things together (Col. 1.17) even when that is not acknowledged. The nearer the centre, the nearer one is to Christ; but the spokes that run out to the rim, which is all-encompassing, are continuous, though those further out may not be as aware of the reality that holds it all together. The earnest desire is that indeed all should recognize the reality and press towards the centre (Phil. 3.12); yet there is still a single whole and each part is needful of the rest, and all are held together in the same loving embrace.

There was also a deepening understanding of the nature of the Kingdom of God. At the heart of the Lord's Prayer we pray, 'your Kingdom come'. We desire the world to be as it is set to be in God's will. The Church is, first of all, a witness to that Kingdom, which though hidden from view and only glimpsed in fragments, shapes all things. The Kingdom is to come in the sense that it will be fully manifest in God's good time, yet it already is present in God's gentle providence. So, in the mystery of God's activity,

creation and history are not beyond God's healing and care. It is
to be part of that Kingdom, therefore, when serving the vision of
a shared humanity, to be committed to justice and peace and to
live in community. Therefore signs of the Kingdom may be found
anywhere, even where the Kingdom may be unknown or even
denied.

From all this came a heightened sense that St Thomas', with
their ecumenical partners, was not simply a small, insignificant
group of people on the fringes of local day-to-day life in Ivytown.
They were, even if not very numerous or weighty, players in a
wider game (1 Cor. 1.26–31). And they had a distinctive witness
to bear. They were commissioned to play their part in local community building, one of the partners in the common life. There
was no need to be ashamed of the gospel, if that set them free to
be fully human alongside, with and for others. Many of the congregation were surprised to learn how widely they were welcomed
in the neighbourhood, among the civic authorities, the schools
and social services. Moreover, once they had taken stock, they
were able to rejoice in how widespread was the network of which
they were a part. Not only were Barbara and Jim involved in a
whole range of organizations and networks, many of their own
members were also key people in various community structures.

Inter-faith encounters

It was not possible to consider St Thomas' place in Ivytown
without looking at relationships with other faith communities,
especially the large Muslim presence. The approach to this issue,
Barbara decided, should, following on from the previous discussions, begin with the experience of the congregation. In any case
she had found that much of what she had come across in her
theological reading on Christian attitudes to other faiths, while
useful as background, was far too theoretical and abstract. For the
people of St Thomas', living with other faiths is an everyday
occurrence and a living issue. The first thing, therefore, was to be
reminded that some of the organizations that use the centre were
run by and for members of other faiths and that members of those
faiths also joined in various other activities. There was, thus,
already a very real point of contact. Members of the congregation,
too, naturally encountered people from different ethnic groups as
neighbours, at the school gate, in shops, and some professionally,

as clients. For a considerable number this was more than casual acquaintance, having visited homes and got to know families and even, in a few cases, attended marriage and funeral ceremonies. Then there were always the festivals and fasts of which the children were particularly aware, learning about them at school, some of which were also very visible on the streets. Barbara and Jim, with the parish priest, had begun to get to know some of their leaders, especially of the gurdwara, occasionally meeting to discuss common concerns in the neighbourhood.

Barbara was pleased to find that, while some, especially the elderly, were anxious and even resentful of the changes in the area, there was little, if any, outright hostility. Rather, there was a desire to build on contacts already made. Slowly, barriers were slipping. There was a strong recognition of the common humanity all shared which should go deeper than any differences. Many were already enjoying the variety that had been introduced, from new foods to different cultural activities.

It was also interesting to learn of the problems faced by members of other communities. Many of them were very familiar: jobs, money, housing, family ties and the generation gap. But all these were exacerbated by their being strangers, having to struggle to find an identity in a new cultural setting. Nor were these groups homogeneous, displaying within themselves national, ethnic, religious and class differences.

Against this background St Thomas' reaffirmed its positive regard for members of other faiths and a policy of appropriate collaboration. That still left, however, the problem of how, as Christians, to view the relation between Christianity and other faiths. It was while discussing this that Barbara found the standard analytical model a useful tool for helping her congregation to sort out their own thinking, though it by no means gave a straightforward answer.

There were, not unexpectedly, some, though only one or two, who took an 'exclusivist' position, claiming that Christianity was the only true religion. It was certainly an attitude found strongly in the independent evangelical congregation and, in a pragmatic, less doctrinaire way, in the black-led church. Nor was it a stance, Barbara recognized, that should be lightly dismissed. Christianity has always made universal claims for Christ as the revelation of God. But it had not, until the emergence of what has been called Christendom, been absolutely exclusivist, assuming, in the West

at least, no salvation outside the Church. Rather, there had always
been a strong strand that had recognized truth and wisdom in
religious and philosophic traditions other than its own. More
experientially – and perhaps this was the real force for those who
wanted to go down this line – Christians down the ages had found
a deep and precious faith which they were reluctant to see compromised or down-graded. Barbara had some real sympathy with
that. Moreover, other religions, both East and West, make similar
claims to universal truth. Nor, as was suggested earlier, were
those outside the Christian community wanting Christians to
compromise their faith. In practice neither inter-community
living nor inter-religious dialogue is helped by muffling one's own
beliefs and commitments. Barbara felt, therefore, that it was
important to give weight to this voice.

There were more who could be called 'pluralists'; that is, who
thought all religion to be fundamentally the same, expressed in
different cultural and historical ways. All would lead to the same
end. Margaret, a teacher, pointed out that this was how they were
able to operate in school with assemblies, by stressing what
religions had in common, especially ethically. Indeed, it could be
argued that pragmatically this is the assumption that appears to be
emerging at the public level, as shown in some of the caring professions and the Government's relations with the so-called 'faith
communities'. Again, Barbara saw the strength of this position.
All religions would seem to have some belief in the 'ground of
being' (Tillich) that undergirds natural existence. There are indeed
commonalities, and to work on these might contribute to a more
peaceful human condition. But against this there are stark and
radical differences. It is not obvious that the 'many names of God'
necessarily point to the same thing. Nor is it clear what to include
as religion. Are there to be 'recognized religions'? And what of a
faith that condones practices regarded as harmful? Or is faith
purely personal? And who will be the arbiter as to what to retain
and what to jettison? Perhaps, however, some sociologists are right
and there will emerge, out of the pluralism, a new religious consensus, not this time under one religion but by a convergence of the
leading religious groups around some common values. It is impossible to predict how faiths, which in any case are continuously
changing, will evolve as they learn to live together. The questions
come when it is assumed that all religions ought radically to adapt
to a prescribed model or approach. This surely is a forlorn hope.

Most of the people in the congregation, however, while they rejected a strong exclusivism, wanted to find a way so to understand Christ as to find in him the ultimate ground of their faith while recognizing and affirming the positive and valuable things in other faiths. Indeed, not a few wanted to witness to the real wisdom, truth and virtue which they had already found deepening and broadening their own faith. In fact they found a parallel here with their thinking about community work. Faith in Christ is that which gives sense and direction to their vision and actions. But that also points beyond the Church to the very heart of all things. So it is to be expected that the God they worship, the God of love, will embrace and succour all creation and all history, and be found reflected in many ways in human experience. Christ is indeed essential and focal for faith but does not preclude saving value being given to other religions.

Moreover, there is another dimension that is integral to the Christian faith. Christianity has an eschatological dimension, a future, in which the fullness of God's purposes and reality will finally be revealed. While we have, in Christ, the true pattern of God's dealings with humanity, we do not yet see clearly and there is much that is still to come (1 Cor. 13.12). It should be no surprise, therefore, if we find ourselves enriched, challenged and invigorated in faith in the encounter with those of other faiths.

Such a position, usually called 'inclusivist', has been the focus of much recent theological debate. Compared with the other two approaches it is much broader and open, home to many variations on a theme, ranging from the near exclusivist to some thing very close to pluralism. There is, however, a strong theological tradition in which it is firmly grounded.

It was here that the people of St Thomas' were able to find both a real sense of fundamental commitment to Christ and a freedom to live with their neighbours with integrity and respect. They recognized that the closer one is to Christ, the more it is possible to accept the other in freedom. Here, too, there were two poles to the issue: to find truth both in the Church and beyond. In this it is possible to rejoice and to leave in God's hands how it will all be worked out. John's Gospel provides a mandate for this. The Logos, the Word, has indeed become flesh, visible and concrete (John 1.14). But this Logos permeates all creation and enlightens everyone (John 1.9). The primary imperative of the Church is to point to his presence in the world. Commitment is thus to be centred on Christ as the way (John 14.16) while recognizing that there are many staging posts and dwellings for the Spirit (John 14.2).

Defining a mission stance

This led to the third question. How were the people of St Thomas' to understand mission? Of course it had been in the background of all the discussions so far. But now it was necessary to be explicit and to find an inner coherence for their existence as a Christian fellowship. This was the subject of an intense period of corporate and personal reflection from Easter through Pentecost. Barbara led a group in the preparation of a booklet of Bible readings, meditations and prayers for use in private devotions. The theme was sustained in the preaching and Bible study sessions. It culminated in an evening conference when the threads were drawn together and woven into a mission statement.

To the surprise of some, such an exercise was in fact a revision course on the whole of the Christian faith: not merely a description of the Church and a programme for action. For they started with God – the *missio Dei* – and the whole sweep of creation, salvation and fulfilment. This was brought home most clearly in a meditation on Rublev's famous icon of *The Old Testament Trinity* – the three figures seated outside Abraham's tent. Here the artist has caught the dynamic of the life of God in the mystery of the three persons who relate to each other in perfect giving and receiving, a community that is one and yet three. But the circle is not complete because it includes the onlooker. God's love spills out into creation and redemption and we are caught up into that life of God that is symbolized by the chalice of communion that is set between the three figures.

Here they began to find the rhythm that informs all Christian existence. But there is need to be more particular. What is our specific mission, here in this time and place? This led to a discussion of the *missiones Dei* – the way the grace of God is to be found at many layers and levels, using many instruments, both secret and open (1 Peter 4.10). So they began to list the ways that they found themselves participating in the *missio Dei*. First, they are all neighbours, living, working and participating alongside others. To be a good neighbour – responsible, reliable, friendly, caring – was seen as a primary Christian witness. But then they are part of a visible institution that bears the name of its Lord, a place of meeting and an active body in the neighbourhood, playing its part in making Ivytown a vibrant and rich community.

Is there not, however, something more? The Church's task is to bear witness to Christ. To borrow from Peter again, it is to give an account of 'the hope that is within you' (1 Peter 3.15). This too is many sided. There is the eucharistic life of thanksgiving for the love of God found in Christ, the quality of the fellowship and the gift of trust and the grace of living. This, it is hoped, will shine through all those activities that are so often thought of as service. Evangelism and service are not separated. Yet evangelism itself is that activity that calls others to faith, to discover with us what gives meaning and purpose and coherence to those who have been found by Christ. This is at the heart of the life of the Church. But it is not simple, for Christ comes to each in their own particularity. Christ has to be presented, whether through proclamation or in the intimacy of the small group or conversation in such a way that he can be found in and for those that seek. Moreover, the disciple has constantly to learn to find Christ anew and to be led into new paths. Evangelism is not a single event but a pilgrimage into which everyone is invited to join.

To be an open church, therefore, is to have a firm and clear centre. In their reflection the congregation had rediscovered their anchor in Christ; that he is able to sustain and empower them. They were emboldened to deepen their witness. At the same time it had been a learning experience, meeting Christ anew, often in strange garb and saying new things and rediscovering things that had been forgotten. Here was a different Lord, yet one who is strangely familiar. At the celebratory dinner that ended the process, member after member, during the round-table time of sharing, expressed gratitude for what they had found – of themselves, of each other, of the vision ahead and, above all, of God.

Barbara, in her sermon the next morning, summed it up. Christ is central. Our eyes have constantly to be turned on him. But he is beyond us and we have only begun the pilgrimage. We have continuously to learn from him and of him. Perhaps what has happened is that there will be a greater consciousness of the 'cosmic' Christ who is the source of all things and fills all things (Eph. 1.22–23). In our walk with Christ we will be more ready to find him at the unexpected moment (Luke 24.13–35). We will be more willing to be led down unlikely paths, with caution perhaps but without fear (John 21.15–19). And this Lord stretches his hand of mercy, wisdom, knowledge and grace over all (Rom. 1.19-20). Together we are called to become human, which is to be called into the fullness of Christ (Eph. 4.13).

Barbara projected three images on the screen to illustrate her point. The first was Grünewald's altarpiece that was so iconic for Karl Barth. John the Baptist points to the crucified Christ. That, said Barth, is the image of the Church, to point away from itself to the Saviour. Faith is not about ourselves or our actions, or even of others, but looking to the source of hope and strength which has been given for the whole world (John 1.35). Evangelism, said D.T. Niles, is one beggar telling another where to find bread. The second was Salvador Dali's *Christ of St John of the Cross*, in which the crucified Christ looks down with love and longing on the world – a world, unlike the empty landscape of the original, busy with all its joys and sorrows, its brokenness and glory. The third was a Masai Christ, an icon by Robert Lentz, of the Good Shepherd. In this simple picture an African, who is Christ in a different culture, is present in a world that is alien to us yet one that we can recognize. These were the elements that were at the heart of their mission statement.

Post-modernism

This chapter set out to illustrate how a congregation can reflect on its own journey and recast and affirm its fundamental theological stance. Of course this is but one story. The other congregations in Ivytown would have come up with variations on the theme. And still others will have very different stories to tell as each tries to be loyal to the calling of Christ in its own place. Christ can be served in many ways and has need of many witnesses. Disappointment comes when these differences of style and circumstances are turned into conflict and schism.

It has been set, however, in the context of one of the major issues that face the Church today – cultural pluralism and inter-faith encounter – without doing more than indicating the complexity of the situation. This situation is, however, a particular expression of what has become widely known as post-modernism. The term points to the radical pluralism that is said to characterize contemporary Western society, together with intra-cultural changes that have further contributed to social fragmentation.

The marks of post-modernism include, therefore, not only ethnic, cultural and religious pluralism but also a hyper-individualism, the collapse of authority, an emphasis on choice and consumerism and, metaphysically, the loss of 'meta-narrative' that gives shape and coherence to society. As part of this, religion, and, in the West, Christianity in particular, it is argued, has become marginalized, relegated to the private and personal. Indeed, the dominant religious discourse would seem to be of a personal spirituality of self-fulfilment found through eclectic experience, picked at will from the range of faiths on offer.

This has clearly become an issue for church life and pastoral practice. But, just as there are controversies about how to understand and assess the signs that give rise to the post-modernist thesis, so there are varied reactions as to what it might imply for the Church. For too many it has been a time of retreat, often into a ghetto which gets ever smaller. Increasingly, however, the postmodern world is being taken seriously. Many others, therefore, have welcomed the situation, seeing in it a new freedom for the Church, which need no longer be constrained by the Enlightenment enterprise. In a world of competing narratives the Church can sell its wares on the open market. What the Church has to do, it is suggested, is to find new patterns of being Church and models of discipleship that meet the challenges of this brave new world.

A different response, however, was indicated by the people of St Thomas'. They recognized the diversity and the problems it causes but would also want to argue that any human society needs to have a degree of social cohesion that is more than mutual convenience or social rivalry that is only held together *in extremis* by plain coercion. Even if the old meta-narratives have retreated they are still there and are a resource for the future. There are churches, mosques and other expressions of cultural and faith traditions. There is no point in being ashamed of one's heritage. But at the same time there is need to be ready to explore and look out for signs of a new pattern that may give order and shape to a society in radical transition. In fact, some would suggest, there are already signs that this is being shaped up. Globalization, for all its ambiguity and harsh injustices, affects us all. Also, there seems to be emerging a renewed place for religion in society, albeit under some hesitancy and confusion. Such a process will take time and patience and cannot be hurried. It may be generations before a new story emerges. Meanwhile we must be getting on with community building, making the bricks out of the straw we possess. In such a fluid situation there is inevitable diversity in experience and practice. The secret is to live faithfully in hope and patience, believing that the God of the past journey will be there in the future (Rom. 5.3–5).

The search for the foundations and models of mission are signs of these changing circumstances. What has been suggested here is that any concept of mission that is worthy of itself must be soundly based on God's will in Christ, for which the Church is not an end in itself but is there for God and the world. It is within this compass that evangelism, witness, Christian nurture, pastoral care, community work and social responsibility combine to serve the greater end which is the Kingdom of God.

Chapter 11

From reflection to action

'Okay, so what shall we do about it?' That was the vicar's question to the main church committee. The organist, a good and godly man, had simply had enough of the awkwardness of the choir, and in his letter to the vicar said that either they gave the choir a break, drew up some new conditions of membership and started again, or he would resign. It was the latest chapter in a series of difficult events surrounding the choir, and the committee was in a mood for action. 'Back the organist,' they said, and they did. There was uproar. 'Choir sacked!' said the newspapers. 'Choir tired and given a rest – says vicar'. And then the cartoonists waded in with their drawings of sleeping choirs and droning preachers. Even network radio got hold of it, and the leader column in a national broadsheet. Meanwhile, back in the parish, there was polite mayhem, anger and resentment on all sides. It was clearly a classic pastoral disaster.

The vicar had broken one of the cardinal rules of pastoral care and practical theology – failing to think through the whole process. In a crisis he was panicked into making a swift, unthinking response. It was a problem that needed instant 'fixing'. In terms of the pastoral cycle he had jumped straight from the experience to the action, without pausing at the vital stages of exploration and reflection. A cooler response would have asked a whole range of questions. What's really going on here? What's the psychological dynamic this group is trapped in? What are the guidelines on conflict management which should be useful here? What are the issues of power and consultation? There were theological issues here too. How is the reign of God going to be evidenced in this situation? What priorities in worship are being demonstrated by the participants in the drama, and what models of the Church are operative? And when all is said and done, what is the Christ-like response here?

The importance of completing the pastoral cycle

If the pastoral cycle is cut short in order to get into the action stage quickly, the possibilities of disaster are greatly magnified; and yet the cycle must reach a particular outcome in practical action. Practical theology is never an abstract and disembodied enterprise; it always, to use the phrase of James Whitehead, moves 'towards some graceful action'.[1] Of course the grace in this action may not be comfortable. Laurie Green gives a sharper definition of what may be expected of the Church and its practice when he writes of it being 'theologically committed to action in matters of justice, peace and community'.[2] Action of this kind often finds friends in odd places and loses them in familiar ones. However, it is of the nature of a praxis approach to ministry that action and reflection, theory and practice, live in mutual support and critique. Faith without works is as dead as a faith which has been reduced to works alone.

Practical theology, then, points to the inescapably practical outcome of the theological enterprise, and this is the fourth phase of the pastoral cycle which we are following through in these chapters. Theology talking to itself demonstrates a sad parody of a high calling, which is to inform and energize the people of God for faithful living. It may not be entirely unfair to claim Jesus as the seminal practical theologian who combined profound reflection with committed action. His example is our mandate.

To raise the stakes a bit higher we may say that the practical outcome we are anticipating from the pastoral cycle is an expression of the mission of God. The characteristic action of the Church is mission because the character of God is fundamentally missiological. Mission is not one activity among others in which the Church engages. The *missio Dei* is of the essence of the Church. This means that the outcome we would expect from the pastoral cycle is one which embodies the loving action of God moving out into his creation in continual renewal and redemption.

In terms of the pastoral cycle, we are on the move in mission from reflection to action. Some practical theologians build in an

intervening stage, that of understanding. The result of the reflective phase of the cycle is the generating of new understanding, a
new theoretical base for further action. This generalizing of new
theory out of the interplay of multidisciplinary exploration and
theological reflection, may look in one of two directions. Conceptually it can remain in the reflection phase, or it can belong to
the action phase. In other words, it may be seen as the result of
theological reflection, a provisional conclusion arising out of the
reflective process which gives the person or group a new way of
looking at the initial situation. On the other hand, it might be
regarded as a springboard to the next phase, that of new action
arising out of the whole cycle of experience–exploration–reflection. How this phase is viewed conceptually does not greatly
matter. The important point is that this encapsulation of a new
vision or understanding is a bridging activity in the missiological
move from reflection to action.

Distortions of the cycle

It must be remembered that the cycle is not a single discrete
event, but part of a spiral of action and reflection leading to new
action and further reflection. We do not come to it innocent of
values and prejudices, nor do we have to embark on the cycle at
the same point each time: we may join a group at its reflection
phase, although that in another sense becomes our initial experience. The point to be made is that the cycle is not unitary and
tidy.

That is not to say, however, that the cycle can be short-
circuited. However many complications and multiplications it
contains, it should be completed. The problem more often is that
there is some distortion of the process by the omission of a vital
stage. Typically these distortions are of three kinds.

From experience to exploration – and no further
When a group of Christians encounter a problem in the life of the
community in which they are set, it is natural for them to seek to
understand it better in order to establish in what ways they might
contribute to the meeting of that problem. It may be a problem of
unemployment following large-scale redundancies at a major
local firm, or a steep rise in homelessness among young people,
or a great sea of loneliness on a particular private estate. The

difficulty often is that the group of Christians, inadequately resourced in time or information, casts around in a well-meaning but aimless way and becomes increasingly frustrated. It seems impossible to get hold of the situation in a manageable way, people are highly pressurized in their own jobs and at church, and the initiative runs into the sands. Experience leads to exploration and that leads nowhere.

Another version of this distortion of the pastoral cycle occurs when the group becomes very involved in exploring the issue but awareness seems itself to be the end of the exercise. A group comes to understand something of the complex aid, trade and debt relationships between the West and the two-thirds world. Avidly it starts to gather information, to watch videos, to set up meetings with London-based 'experts'. There is an attempt to get fact-sheets into the pews and to set up an exhibition in the church foyer. However, summer comes, enthusiasm begins to wane, and only the die-hard convenor is left by the autumn. A worthy response runs out of energy, because anchoring that response in the demands of the gospel and working out the implications in the costly obedience of practical action in the community and beyond, prove to be further than the group's commitment could reach. The pastoral cycle is aborted.

From experience to reflection in one move – and no further
Another distortion of the cycle is to take the issue into the church's Christian education programme and leave it there. This is the distortion which omits the exploration stage, believing that there are proper and sufficient Christian answers to these difficult life issues. It may also be hoped that the discussion of them will somehow deflect the guilt they engender. When the problem of unemployment comes up in the church it is too easy to make it part of a sermon or study course on contemporary problems for which the Bible has the right principles and answers. The hard analytical work of understanding the complex economic and social issues is the casualty.

The error is compounded when subsequently the church also omits the action stage because the issue was subject to Christian domestication in the house group and lost its power to energize a practical response. It's impossible to know what an adequate response would be like apart from the actual situation, but at least there may be research to do on local training initiatives, job clubs and advice centres, to which the church might contribute practical help. Projects part-financed by Church Urban Fund money have breathed new hope into many corners of despair throughout the country.

The first error, in omitting the exploration stage, is incarnational; it fails to recognize that God is able to disclose his presence and truth in the disciplines of the secular order, as well as through the revelatory clarity of Scripture and tradition. The second error, in neglecting the action stage, is redemptive; vital issues in society such as race, gender, homophobia and homelessness are not in themselves redeemed by Bible study and prayer, unless Christians are open to that radical obedience to Scripture and the call of God which will drive them into action. Salvation by small groups is not a methodology Amos would have recognized.

From experience to action – with nothing in between
This was the distortion of the pastoral cycle exhibited by the vicar with his choir at the start of the chapter. It was the classic knee-jerk response of the hard-pressed minister. Here was a problem to sort out; there was no time for the kind of considered reflection you talked about at theological college; bringing theology to bear on the situation seemed both self-indulgent and too complex; it was just a situation that needed firm handling. However, a little time spent in cool exploration and reflection would have saved a vast amount of time mopping up the spilt blood of a pastoral nightmare. The challenge of theological education to the trainee minister is to prepare not just for ministry but for thoughtful ministry. The charge of activism is one often brought by clergy against themselves, but the alternative proves elusive. That alternative is of reflective activity, meditative engagement, a ministry made up of chosen priorities in line with a theologically informed vision. Such a vision is not realized by hand-to-mouth ministry and the careless abandonment of that proven method in ministry known as the pastoral cycle.

Six types of change

When we consider what type of action or change might result from our model of reflection, there are six major modes of change which may be operational. Rarely will many of these modes be found all happening together, but often there will be more than one type of change taking place. Moreover, it is clear that different situations lend themselves more to one type of change than another.

- **Cognitive change**. Students and others involved in ministry may find that the outcome of the process is mostly at the intellectual level. New things have been learned by the participants about the nature of God, or how society functions in the area of race, or what different people mean by prayer. ('Intellectual' here does not necessarily mean 'academic'; it means the cognitive, thinking dimension of human experience.) If it is argued that this seems to deny the assertion above, that the pastoral cycle is only completed in action, it should be remembered that the process will often go through a number of cycles before final effective action results; but that result would have been impossible without the cumulative learning of the previous turns of the cycle.
- **Affective change**. Change in this mode involves the emotions and the attitudinal change which results from significant experience. Exposure to the pain many women feel at the consistent use of exclusive, male-gendered liturgical language may lead to a shift in someone's attitude and emotional response to particular acts of worship.
- **Behaviourial change**. When new skills are learned through having engaged in an experience which exposed weaknesses or unexamined needs, then these behavioural changes can be immensely rewarding. New competencies emerge which are then affirmed by those who benefit from that competence, be it in taking a funeral service well or successfully tiling the bathroom!
- **Interpersonal change**. These changes are to do with handling oneself in relation to others, both in individual encounter and in groups. It can again be very rewarding when ministers know they have guided a group through a dangerous discussion in such a way that there has been honesty without malice, genuine listening, and the discovery of a constructive way ahead; or when a student feels much more confident in skills of pastoral care as a result of regularly visiting a hospital ward.
- **Social and political change**. This is the type of change which occurs when a person begins to see him or herself not

just as an individual reacting with other individuals, but as part of a community with social and political responsibilities. This sense of existing within the corporate domain and, as a Christian, having a duty of holy obedience in that context, can sometimes be a radical transformation in outlook and motivation, even like a new conversion.

- **Spiritual change**. This is not put last as a perfunctory nod in the direction of religious political correctness. This is the area of unifying change, of a vision and practice which both empowers people of faith and subverts their idols. It is the area of deep, continuous re-formation from which flows (and sometimes erupts) the creative energy to engage in new ways with God's mission in his world. Without it, for the Christian, all other change is relativized.

The range of possible outcomes in the cycle

This typology of change gives us a background to the different possible outcomes in the action phase of our model of practical theology. The following is not exhaustive or the only framework for practical response, but it has the merit of relating constructively to the wider typology above. In outline the range is as follows:

- educational activity
- new attitudes
- refinement of skills
- corrective action
- new action
- prayer and celebration.

Educational activity

We have previously suggested that a purely exploratory or reflective response to a situation in ministry may be a distortion of the pastoral cycle in that it may arrest the movement through to practical action. It may be, however, that an educational, cognitive outcome is appropriate, or at least appropriate to this particular operation of the cycle, with a subsequent run-through leading to a more tangible response. In the example given above, the events set up by the group committed to examining the roots of world poverty may have been entirely right and, for the time being, sufficient in themselves. There is no short cut in the process of learning facts and theories in complex areas so that subsequent action is soundly based.

Educational theory sometimes points to six models of educational process.[3] The minister who wants to help a group through the pastoral cycle will need to be aware of the strengths and weaknesses of these different models, and also of his or her preferences. In this way the minister will be able to make sure that the educational outcome of the cycle is the most effective and appropriate one for the particular group.

- **Liberal education** emphasizes wisdom as the goal, and reason as the method of attaining it. The educated person is best described as 'knowledgeable' because he or she has received information transmitted by those with special expertise. Typical formats would be: a lecture, a panel of experts, or a structured home learning course.

- **Progressive education** emphasizes social and individual change as the goal, and problem-solving and guidance as the method of attaining it. Knowledge is about exercising good judgement, and education works by a process of problem-solving, the learner taking responsibility for his or her own learning. The aim is often to bring about specific change or social improvement, and so the process is usually activist and democratic in nature.

- **Humanistic education** emphasizes integration and wholeness as the goal, and facilitation and support as the method of getting there. What matters most is a growing self-knowledge. Such a process might be seen in a training course for pastoral care, bereavement visiting or spiritual direction, where the methods used are inductive and participatory, with people being asked to examine their own condition *vis-à-vis* the pastoral task before turning to the task itself.

- **Technological education** emphasizes efficiency and productivity as the goal, and instruction and moulding as the method of achieving it. The essence of knowledge is performance, and the goal is competence in particular tasks. Typical examples would be training the choir or those who lead intercessions, preparing the youth group to lead a service, or couples to help in marriage preparation. The method is designed to give confidence and to allow people the satisfaction of doing a job well.

*   **Radical education** emphasizes freedom from oppression as the goal, and conscientization and empowerment as the method of attaining it. Knowledge is about reflective thought and action. Personal and social conversion is at the heart of the process, and so people must above all be able to make their own choices. The radical edge of this educational method is hard for established systems to incorporate for it is always subverting the systems themselves! For this reason the Church has found it harder to take it into the centre of its life, leaving it to those important radical groups on its edge which act as its conscience – for example, new forms of community or charities on the margins of society.

*   **Dogmatic education** emphasizes obedience and trust as the goal, and proclamation as the appropriate method to use. Knowledge consists of understanding revealed truth or credal formulae. This method gives certainty and support through imparting clear beliefs and practices. Learning a catechism or an evangelistic method by rote would be examples of this particular approach.

Each of these models has its strengths and its advocates. Progressive, technological and radical education in particular have a practical outcome. Liberal humanistic and dogmatic education, however, see acquired knowledge as valuable in itself, leading to a greater self-awareness and strength and eventually, but not necessarily immediately, to a new form of practice. It is this practical outcome of acquiring knowledge which we are here identifying as the final product of the learning cycle.

If exposure to Hinduism on a trip to India sends someone to study world religions at an adult education class, there is real value in the extension of horizons and sympathies. It may be, however, that a further process of exploration and reflection takes place later which leads in turn to dialogue or common action with other faith communities in the area. The educational process is never finished; it always reaches out to extend itself, and ideally to express itself in particular actions.

With some knowledge of educational theory about teaching and learning methods the minister or lay educator will be better able to further the Church's primary task of mission. He or she will understand what educational goals and methods will be most beneficial in a particular setting, and will be able to move the Church into appropriate action.

New attitudes

This is the form of outcome which corresponds to 'affective change' in our previous typology. In the debate in the Anglican Church on the ordination of women, a clergyman is often heard bearing witness to the change in his attitude which came about from the experience of working alongside a woman in ministry. Cognitive thinking is often complemented, informed, or subverted by the deep shifts in emotional response which practical experience brings about. No one who thinks seriously about ministry can afford to neglect all that mass of the human subconscious, an iceberg which lies mostly submerged from view. It is an area of enormous power, often dressed up as 'respectable theology'.

There is here, of course, a particular link with a habitus approach to practical theology. The task of theology in this framework is to come to 'a personal knowledge of God and of the things of God in the context of salvation'.[4] Theology in this form produces a habit of the human soul, a way of being before God. A significant element in such a theology, therefore, is the realm of attitudes and personal responses to God, to the world, to the Church and to humankind.

At a church weekend away, in an atmosphere of trust and openness, it emerged that James was gay. The church had not had to face the issue of gay Christians before and now set about some hard thinking. Initially James suffered some hurtful judgements and misunderstanding but the church struggled on with its feelings and its theology and came to a new sensitivity which somehow affected all of its relationships and its life together. The outcome of the pastoral cycle was a profound change in attitudes.

Refinement of skills

This is the behavioural response to the learning process. It is one of the tasks and opportunities of the student placement and even more of the minister's first appointment, to allow the student or new minister to learn from the experience of undertaking a host of ministerial tasks with varying degrees of success. For many years there has been a fairly consistent struggle between the perception of the Church at grass roots that theological education should be preparing students for ministry by equipping them with skills and techniques, and the perception of theological educators that their job is to prepare the student by offering a theological framework for the practice of ministry, leaving most skills-training until the first appointment. It is plainly impossible in two or three years of theological education to cover everything necessary for a lifetime's ministry; equally it would be negligent of theological educators not to address the need for skills at all. However, the issue of competence in ministry becomes unavoidable when the actual tasks have to be fulfilled at a particular moment and by a particular person. Learning and refining of skills then becomes the most important outcome of the pastoral cycle.

While not actually going so far as to drop the baby into the font, Adam was dismayed by his performance at his first baptism service. He was unsure of himself; he was completely thrown by the level of noise; his sermon was too long and hopelessly complex. He came out hot and bothered, and determined to do better next time. He talked, read and thought. His theological education was useful, but first he had to think a lot more about what baptism meant to people in this area and what the cultural conventions were with which the church was interacting. A chat with Molly, the church secretary, and Greta, the hall cleaner, were helpful here. They'd had eight children between them, and had lived in the area all their lives. As he began to think again about his lecture notes from college, Adam now began to see them in a different light. He also began to think very hard about sharpening his communication skills. What precisely did he want to say? Indeed, what did he actually need to say? Could he thread his sermon throughout the service rather than deliver it at one point? How would he cope with noise and inattention? What was the demeanour and style that best suited the occasion, rather than his starchy approach, defending the dignity of the sacrament? When the next baptisms came, Adam was much better prepared. He'd worked hard and it went well. He knew he had learned from the experience, but he hoped his first wedding service would not be as bad!

Skills are constantly being refined by the thoughtful practitioner in ministry. Each time a particular skill is employed there is an opportunity to improve on the last time. When a task has been performed twenty times the question to ask is whether it has been repeated nineteen times or refined nineteen times. The minister who has stayed alive in his work is performing the task very differently the twentieth time around.

Corrective action

The difference between Adam's refinement of his skills in baptism and the fourth type of practical response to the pastoral cycle is that the latter – corrective action – is more likely to be corporate and structural in nature. Skills operate more often at the individual level (though not exclusively: it is legitimate to refer to a community's skills in, for example, handling change or conflict). An institution, however, is often likely to have to take corrective action when its structures and practices no longer serve the need for which they were originally designed.

It may be that a church has to overhaul its committee structure as a result of an audit or a review. There may need to be a new policy on marriage preparation since those responsible for working the existing scheme have moved on and taken the impetus with them. Church youth work often seems to be in need of corrective action as the youth scene in the local church, and in society as a whole, changes in focus and style.

When we view the almost constant change in the institutions and structures of industry and society in recent decades, it should come as no surprise that our own structures often stand in need of revision.[5] The misfortune of the Church is that so often change is seen as threat, and innovation as gimmickry.

New action

The outcome of the cycle of practical theology is often new activity in or by the church as it pursues its mission. The action may be ecclesial or social, personal or political, but it will involve going through the process of thinking out exactly what is necessary and how it will be achieved. Churches have a sorry history of setting up new activities without very thorough preparation in theology, consultation, practical detail or possible consequences. If, however, the pastoral cycle has been properly followed there are at least good grounds to hope that the new action will be coming out of a thoughtful process of examination and discernment.

At this stage there are two sets of questions which remain to be asked:

(1)   Is the action theologically justified?
(2)   Is the action thoroughly and systematically planned?

Laurie Green offers helpful criteria for the first question.[6] He suggests that any theological enterprise should have the purpose of being

- contemplative
- instructive
- transformative.

To be contemplative is not to be quietist but to be able to discern the presence and activity of God more readily and to respond in love. An action informed by theology will be instructive inasmuch as it offers the opportunity to learn and grow in the life and truth of God, and to be more attuned to his purposes. To be transformative an action will be contributing to the restructuring of the present, in line with the hopes and longings of the Kingdom of God. Even when the learning cycle has yielded the particular result of a proposed form of new action, these questions must still be put to it. Is the action theologically based, or simply a 'good idea'?

If this begins to answer the first question, of whether the action is theologically justified, there is another set of questions which must also be asked, this time to do with the implementation of the proposed action. Is there a systematic, planned approach to the new activity? A straightforward checklist of necessary steps can save later descent into chaos.

- **Aim**. Until this is crystal clear, no further action should be taken. The best way then to check that this clarified aim is well grounded in the missionary purposes of God is to go on asking of that aim the question 'why?' There should be a clear line of consistency and coherence between the stated aim and the ultimate theological vision.
- **Information**. All information which might be at all relevant to the proposed action should be gathered, recorded and shaped, as outlined in Chapter 7. If, for example, a bereavement visiting group is being set up, relevant information will include: the number of funerals, current pastoral practice, possible training courses, good practice

elsewhere, insights on bereavement from psychology and sociology, and more.

- **Areas of action**. A list must be produced of what has to be done, in general outline. For the bereavement visiting group this might include: recruitment to the team of visitors, appropriate training, communication of the scheme to the church, communication to the bereaved (including support-ive literature), leadership and co-ordination, continuing support to visitors, etc.

- **Plan**. The next stage is the formulation of a specific plan, taking into account the areas of necessary action above. The plan should be concrete and timetabled, and make clear who is responsible for what action and to whom they are accountable. As with the aim, lack of clarity at this point creates the possibility of subsequent mayhem!

- **Action**. The plan is implemented according to the agreed timeframe and by the designated people. Implementation may be phased so that particular targets are met sequen-tially.

- **Review**. This essential stage is so often omitted. The group responsible for the new action must build in a review timetable within the plan itself. The review may take place on the completion of the task, during the phased implemen-tation of the task, or in the ongoing monitoring of the project. The review represents the first stage of a new run-through of the learning cycle. Vital lessons are there to be learned from the implementation of the plan in the action stage which will refine and improve the project. Without it, of course, history will repeat itself.

This systematic, planned approach to new action as a result of the pastoral cycle is an important tool to have available and to use. There are, however, many other tools in the toolbox! Some understanding of the dynamics of structural change is of great value.[7] It is also important to be aware of models for handling conflict, and here, for example, the force-field analysis of Kurt Lewin can prove useful.[8]

These and other analytical tools from the human and manage-ment sciences are there for Christians to use appropriately in order to secure, under God, the best possibility of success for the new enterprise. 'Success' in the context of a Kingdom ruled by a

'God who died' is bound to be a concept with a complex character. Nevertheless we owe it to the risen and ascended Lord to seek
to achieve what we perceive to be God-directed goals. But how do
we discern what is 'God-directed'? This brings us to our sixth type
of action resulting from the pastoral cycle.

Prayer and celebration
In our typology of change this clearly corresponds to the spiritual
mode of response. It is not reducible simply to the affective or
behavioural modes; it is both cognitive and interpersonal, but
more than either; it may well incorporate or inspire social and
political change, but it is larger than both. It may well be that the
most appropriate response to the engagement of the methods of
practical theology to a particular situation, is simply to pray,
though with a mind and heart more informed, aware and sensitive. Our theological journey may have disclosed to us the
presence and action of God in unexpected ways and we may
decide that he is handling it perfectly well! Our prayer then
associates us with his graceful activity and opens us to new
promptings of the Holy Spirit for our own involvement. Alternatively we may find that the response drawn from us is one of
thankfulness and joy, and our best action is to celebrate all that is
good in the situation in worship, festival, party and song. These
are themes we will explore further in the next chapter.

Continuing the cycle of practical theology

It may be true that 'we brought nothing into the world and it is
certain that we shall carry nothing out' (1 Tim. 6.7); nevertheless in the meantime we bring plenty of baggage into any new
situation and we take even more out of it! We do not enter the
learning cycle with a blank sheet of experience, available for anything to be written upon us. We come with a backlog of attitudes,
prejudices, understandings and intuitions which between them
create a powerful filter for the new experience to which we are
exposed. Our pre-understanding determines what it is that we
observe, what we accept as valid evidence, and what we regard as
significant.

Equally, at the far end of the cycle, we take a refined understanding or a new approach or a reshaped world view, into new
situations or missionary actions. And that in itself provides the

new filter with which we enter the next turn of the cycle. The process is continuous and developmental. In that sense, practical theology is an eschatological discipline. It reaches out to the final vision of the Kingdom to which all things are drawn by the God who inhabits the future. The works of ministry are both relativized and enhanced by that vision. They are both interim activities awaiting the fulfilment of all things in Christ, and also activities of supreme importance because they act as signs of the Kingdom already present and active, the first fruits of the age to come.

To fail to move on and continue the process of action and reflection in the missionary service of Christ would be to deny our belief in the coming Kingdom.

Notes

1   Whitehead, J., 'The Practical Play of Theology' in Mudge, L. and Poling, J., eds, *Formation and Reflection* (Fortress Press 1987), p. 47.
2   Green, L., *Let's Do Theology* (Mowbray 1990), p. 100.
3   For example: *Christian Education and Training for the 21st Century*, General Synod Misc. 389, 1992; Craig, Y., *Learning for Life* (Mowbray 1994), ch. 2.
4   Farley, E., *Theologia* (Fortress Press 1992). See also his definitions on p. 35: 'a habit, an enduring orientation and dexterity of the soul', 'a cognitive disposition and orientation of the soul, a knowledge of God and what God reveals'.
5   A reliable mapmaker in the field is Charles Handy. See *The Empty Raincoat* (Hutchinson 1994). The organization MODEM is committed to dialogue between the worlds of management and the Church, a dialogue which is being increasingly constructive in the field of leadership. See also: John Adair and John Nelson, *Creative Church Leadership* (Canterbury 2004) and Malcolm Terry, *Managing God's Business* (Ashgate 2006), but for a word of caution Stephen Pattison, *The Faith of the Managers* (Cassell 1997).
6   Green, op. cit., p.105.
7   Blake, R. and Mouton, J., *Advanced Management Office Executive*. 1962, further developed in *The New Managerial Grid*. 1978. Their grid has been adapted to many different situations, including management in ministry.
8   Kurt Lewin's helpful approach of 'force-field analysis' crops up in many different settings, showing itself to be an effective multidisciplinary tool.

Chapter 12

A spirituality equal to the task

The purpose of the pastoral cycle is not to make theological technicians. All that has gone before in this book might give the impression that the chief aim of a model of practical theology is simply to enable those involved in ministry to find their way successfully through a theological process. The true aim, however, is rather different: it is to enable those involved in ministry to come to an informed pastoral wisdom based on the knowledge of God.

We are back here with the concept of habitus, mentioned in Chapters 4 and 5. Habitus is that disposition of the mind and heart from which all Christian action flows. It is a way of being before God and with others such that the responses of Christian discipleship are made holistically and wisely. It engages the whole personality, holding together the reasons of both spiritual wisdom and intellectual commitment. It is not a short cut in pastoral ministry, a final abdication of responsibility for hard thinking and analysis. Rather it is the goal and context for all that work, the personal orientation which gives direction to the will.

The pastoral cycle, therefore, is merely a particular method which contributes to the development in God's people of a practical Christian instinct. From who we are comes what we do. And we become who we are by exposure to the Christian story and the demands of discipleship. When we hear the parable of the Good Samaritan for the hundredth time, we are almost certainly not gaining new information, but we are being fed and watered by it. Its function is 'performative' rather than 'informative'. How we respond to the story in the practice of our discipleship will then reinforce our basic habitus. Thus we establish our identity as Christians by living under the influence of the basic stories of the faith. In this way the Body of Christ is formed as a community with a particular character[1] and with 'characteristic' ways of responding to the challenges and needs of society.

If the overall purpose of a model of practical theology, therefore, is to facilitate habitus, a disposition of mind and heart characterized by informed Christian wisdom, another question begins to emerge: what kind of spiritual practice and discipline is equal to the task of nourishing a 'practical theologian', that is, any Christian involved in active ministry? Are there distinctive marks of a spirituality which would undergird the kind of ministerial engagement we have been describing? Equally, is there a way of being before God in prayer and celebration which not only supports this ministry but is created by it? It is inevitably the case that our ways of prayer and reflection do not emerge in a social vacuum. They are the product of a complex interplay of personal, cultural and theological factors, not the least of which is how we characteristically act in ministry and with what effect. Our experience of God's presence and activity in the Church and in society is bound to affect the way we pray.

In seeking to identify some distinctive marks of a spirituality which supports and nourishes practical ministry there is an obvious danger. It is tempting to suggest that only this one particular form of spirituality which we identify is appropriate to the task. We must beware of the tendency to off-load our prejudices about spirituality by making extravagant claims for our own preferences. We have to recognize as valid any form of prayer and reflection which effectively supports men and women in their discipleship. As we have continually maintained, everyone is their own practical theologian if they are thoughtfully engaged in ministry; and everyone's way of finding and being found by God is therefore to be taken seriously. Nevertheless, there is some value in taking the risk of identifying a number of key elements of a working spirituality which may be appropriate to the task of practical theology.

A spirituality which is biblical and radical

There are many ways of using the Bible which are comforting and reassuring; there is a long tradition of treating the Bible as a sweet factory. There is, however, just as long a tradition of seeing the Bible as a radical, challenging and often subversive document, used by God to unsettle his people even as he assures them of his steadfast love. This is the tradition which recognizes the Scriptures as 'sharper than a two-edged sword' (Heb. 4.12), and the message of Jesus as bringing 'not peace on earth but rather division' (Luke 12.51). No Western reader of the prophets, the Magnificat, or Jesus' condemnation of the professionally religious (Matt. 23) can come away feeling comfortable.

This tradition of Bible reading has been followed up in recent times by writers such as David Sheppard, Charles Elliott, Gerard Hughes, Jim Wallis and others – all taking the Scriptures with genuine seriousness in order to let God speak to contemporary society.[2] This is also the task of the base communities in South America where biblical texts can have an edge rarely experienced in the first world.[3] Liberation perspectives have also found their way into Bible study methods in Britain so that text and context can more closely relate to each other and lead to practical action.[4] This biblical radicalism is the spirit of Greenbelt, the annual arts festival which regularly faces the difficult issues of culture and change, politics and prayer with an openness born of confidence in biblical wisdom and authority.

Some theological colleges have centres for urban studies where students can live for a period and do their study in a different context and style from their college. To read the sermon on the mount in a tower block in Gateshead is to have a different set of questions asked of the reader, and will produce a different set of emotional responses to the text. The crucial questions of our time, whether they be about urban deprivation, third world debt, ozone depletion or ethnic warfare, are unlikely to be addressed sharply enough by the conventional biblical exegesis offered to suburban churches in the home counties. The deeper, unsettling consequences of a riskier hermeneutic, however, can engage these issues in a way which revitalizes the Church's confidence in its biblical heritage.

A spirituality which is socially and politically earthed

It follows from taking the Bible as a radical document that a spirituality which resources, and is resourced by, the practice of ministry will also be one which embraces community and social action. The division between sacred and secular finally breaks down. Personal faith and social action are indivisible.

As Archbishop Desmond Tutu memorably said: 'I wonder which Bible some people are reading when they tell me that religion and politics do not mix.' Or, as Ken Leech observes: 'Christianity goes disastrously and dangerously wrong when Jesus is worshipped but not followed.'[5] The following of Jesus will take Christians into the struggle for what he called 'the weightier matters of the law: justice and mercy and faith' (Matt. 23.23).

Many a congregation has found that when it focuses on particular needs in the community and tries to make a response in line with gospel imperatives, its quality of life benefits in an extraordinary way. Worship seems more vital, relationships closer, God's presence more tangible. If the church is establishing day care provision for the elderly or clubs for latch-key children; if the congregation is struggling with the funding of a community worker or battling to raise the morale of a depressed estate; then there can be a new sense of conviction in the church and a fresh confidence in its mission. The deeper reason is that these actions are reflecting the values of the Kingdom of God and therefore have a more profound mandate.

Two of the books which have recently helped British Christians to hold together prayer and social action in a rich interdependence have been Charles Elliott's *Praying the Kingdom* and Gerard Hughes' *God of Surprises*.[6] Both have encouraged Christians to go more deeply into the resources of imaginative prayer and to take the issues of peace and justice as normative concerns. This interaction has about it the ring of truth. Brother Roger of Taizé wrote much about the dialectic between struggle and contemplation, which also fired the prophetic heart and pen of Thomas Merton.

Moreover fresh outrage draws out fresh theological reflection. Miroslav Volf, in his *Exclusion and Embrace*,[7] writes out of the suffering of his people in the Balkans, challenging the tragic hatreds of exclusion with the embrace that lies at the heart of the gospel. The argument of this book involves rich theology, historical vision and human insight, together shaping a truly Christian response to the prevailing violence of our times. Volf wrote the book as a struggle that was both intellectual and spiritual, and it emerges as both theological and political.

We have only to consider the alternative to this earthy spirituality to see how central it must be to authentic Christian existence. Laurie Green uses the following picture in *Let's Do Theology*,[8] attributing it to a Latin American source. The Church in this analogy is represented by a wonderful car which is kept by a family in the large garage of their suburban home. They visit it regularly to admire it and polish it, but they never take it out on the dirty and dangerous roads. On Sundays the family make up a picnic and go and spend the day in the car in the garage, and sing rather sentimental songs there about journeys and dangers on the roads and the beauty of their car. Twice a year they have a special car festival and invite their neighbours to come into the garage with them, where they open presents and try to make the garage welcoming. The family is much loved and respected by their friends and neighbours. Sadly, though, everyone knows the family is insane.

The Church is indeed a very special vehicle but it only exists to move on the 'dirty and dangerous' roads where the Kingdom of God has to be shaped. As a sacrament of the Kingdom, the Church has the highest of callings. If it fails to live by that calling and instead amuses itself in the garage, then the tragedy is complete. A spirituality which serves the mission of God, therefore, inevitably has an earthy, social dimension. Moreover, it will not be concerned with defending its boundaries, keeping its life from dirt and danger on the roads. Indeed it will seek 'contaminating contact' with the world for which Christ died, for there the struggle for life rather than death is keenest, and there the liberating story of Jesus will be heard most clearly.

A spirituality which engages with suffering and celebrates resurrection

Again, it follows from this earthiness that our habitus spirituality will lead us into life's hard places where the motifs of cross and resurrection will continually echo. The experience of those who truly enter life's danger zones is that they are thrown ever more deeply into the mystery of a suffering God but that their special privilege is to point to the further truth of Christ risen and ascended behind the darkness.

In church life we sometimes come across faces which are full of suffering, but full also of the overcoming of that suffering. These are the saints of the journey who may, if coaxed, tell others something of what they have learnt. However, there is another level of more normal Christian existence which is unafraid to face

difficulties and painful issues because this is the path the
Kingdom-bearer himself took. There are those in the church
therefore who will take on regular work in the night shelter or the
hospice, or who will take their faith into the grey compromises of
local politics. There are those who care endlessly for relatives with
senile dementia and those who give themselves to the victims of
despair, racism or violent crime. The arenas are endless, and the
sustaining grace for selfless identification with those who hurt is
found in the dark cross of Golgotha and the indestructible light of
Easter morning. Ministers of Christ, lay or ordained, are constantly forced back into this crucible of pain and joy, and spend
much time meditating on the paschal mystery.

What has to be avoided, however, is a false cheapening of the
cross and a domestication of resurrection. A minister who fails to
get his own way or whose stubbornness leads him into conflict,
should claim some identification with a mule, not with the cross!
The resurrection is a sign of the renewal of all creation and the
language of resurrection should not be too easily commandeered
to describe minor personal success. Nevertheless, the cross and
resurrection will be recurring themes of any spirituality which
takes the exigencies of human experience seriously. The cross
becomes a thing of darkness and tears, a mystery to enter rather
than a formula to understand: and the resurrection is a place of
joy far beyond words. The rest is silence and prayer.

A spirituality which has depth and integrity

No service is done to those truly wrestling with the reality of
human need by offering them services of worship which are little
more than well-packaged Christian entertainment. Some worship
seems to be shaped primarily around the principle that it must
be enjoyable, and not risk challenge or complexity. In fact the
greatest need in worship is depth. We have to be taken beyond
ourselves if we are to encounter God, and this will involve a rich
mix of Word and sacrament, symbol and art form, music and
atmosphere, celebration and silence. We have to be invited into a
bigger space where we might easily become lost. We have to
encounter strangeness which might or might not become discovery. At the same time we have to be in touch with the real world of
men and women. Otherwise worship is in free-fall, unrelated to
anything but our own personal soul-searching. Worship needs

relevance without triviality, depth without abstraction. It is therefore an art form of rare complexity!

What is true of public liturgy is also true of private prayer. Those who are praying and working for the Kingdom need to find ways of being before God which feed and resource the hard work, and which also allow satisfying forms of celebration. Whether this is through Bible study and prayer, a daily office, contemplative silence, or practising the presence of God through the day, does not greatly matter. What does matter, however, is that the individual has both a measure of self-awareness and also a knowledge of the riches of Christian spiritual traditions, which enable him or her to make the necessary connections. Currently, many Christians are being helped in the enterprise of gaining greater self-awareness by the insights of the Myers–Briggs personality type indicator or the ancient Enneagram,[9] which helpfully relate personality and methods of prayer. These are only suggestive tools, not precise instruments, and are meant to liberate people, not to pigeon-hole them. The most they claim is that people may be able to recognize their spiritual 'home' so that they can go out on journeys of the spirit with greater confidence.

In pursuit of the necessary resources for vital Christian living, many are also being helped by the resurgence of the retreat movement, the plethora of books on different forms of spirituality, and the increasing recognition across the church spectrum of the value of spiritual directors or soul friends. What matters finally is that worship and prayer be real and have depth. For the committed believer this is not a trivial pursuit; it is a matter of life or death.

A spirituality which is drawn to the image of journey

A student went to see his tutor with a deep anger. He had come to college with a straightforward, outgoing faith and the enthusiasm to share it. But he had been on two hard placements: one in a home for runaways, the other in a tough working-class parish. And then a homeless alcoholic, whom he had befriended, died alone. He was angry at the Church, at the college, and at himself for being so superficial, as he saw it, for so long. He had changed a lot in two years and now looked at his past faith with something approaching horror.

The tutor listened. Partly he had to absorb the tirade, and

partly he had to interpret it. The student had been on a journey. He could trace his Christian origins back to childhood, and perhaps now he could try and see not just two stages of 'error' and 'truth' but a lifetime of journeying, travelling further into the realm of the reign of God, discovering new layers of truth and meaning in the gospel. Perhaps the other side of anger could be excitement at the new opportunities of serving a God who was even bigger than he had thought.

For this student it was the practicalities of ministry and the use of the pastoral cycle which led him to new places on his Christian journey. In some ways the model of the journey has the feel of a succession of conversions.[10] The first is to an initial living faith and it has about it an idealism and a sense of innocent conviction and certainty which can both attract and repel. Although sometimes this stage of the journey is looked back on with a measure of embarrassment it is a necessary point of entry and very often acts as a kind of touchstone for later experience even if that experience is widely divergent from the original. If that faith is to grow then the initially exuberant but fragile faith will probably encounter doubt as the pain and cost of discipleship begin to mount. The pain may be intellectual, moral or emotional, but it is likely to take someone out into the desert where the real business of discipleship is sorted out.

The desert is in our own soul and involves coming to terms with our own personality and our own past, our fragmentedness and prejudice. Accepting all this as what we are and what we offer to God is the second conversion. As Tillich puts it: we 'accept the fact that we are accepted, even though unacceptable.'[11]

The third conversion is a turning back to the world, recognizing that individuals and groups in society share that same brokenness we have come to see in ourselves. Empowered not by the strength of our own grip on Christ, but rather by an inner waiting and dependence on him and a patient listening for the promptings of the Spirit, we are now able to feel the pulse of the world's life without being tempted to manipulate it. We are now free to be present with others and attentive to them, and so to discern what God is already doing, and to join him in doing it. Ministry is thus rescued from much of its naivety and self-deception, and set free to be more genuinely liberating and transforming of people and situations.

Although this stylized version of the journey may not be the reader's, some form of journey certainly is. However, the model of journeying does not invalidate other metaphors. For example, there is a very important evangelical metaphor of 'arrival' which points to the proper confidence a Christian may have in a God who has done the journeying for us, leaving us only to welcome him. Models can be held in tension as illuminating different facets of the truth, and of course they are only helpful as long as they help! Nevertheless, the metaphor of the journey picks up a central biblical motif and echoes the experience of very many Christian people.

A spirituality which is humble

One element of the humility of a spirituality for ministry has already been touched on above. The third conversion to the world and its pain, which arises out of a recognition of our equal standing in need before God, helps us to sit more attentively with others and to have fewer things to say – though hopefully those fewer things are more valuable.

A minister was once sitting in a small hospital ward talking quietly to a patient when the hospital chaplain came in, unaware that one of the visitors was also ordained. He stood in the middle of the four-bedded room, smiled genially and then spoke at everyone in a succession of Christian generalizations before sweeping out with a general air of bonhomie, leaving the ward stunned. As a form of pastoral care it was inept, embarrassing and patronizing, and it made no attempt to engage with the patients themselves. Humility before human need would have transformed the chaplain's whole approach.

There is another form of humility, however, which a spirituality of ministry requires. This is a humility of status. In particular there is need for the clergy to relinquish their hold upon theology so that it can be reclaimed with confidence by the whole people of God. Ian Fraser called it 'reinventing theology as the people's work'.[12] This is a deeply sacrificial task for clergy who have been used to thinking that this at least is their own special preserve, a body of professional knowledge which can be dispensed and controlled at their will. The pastoral cycle envisages ministers being much more the facilitators and resource people who have a key role in enabling the people of God to do their own theology.

Humility before those in need and before the people of God

can only come from a life of prayer focusing on a God who
himself chose the way of humility, who 'made himself nothing,
taking the very nature of a servant' (Phil. 2.7). In a world where
upward mobility is prized highly, to choose 'downward mobility'
is a courageous act. Clergy and laity need to be gentle with each
other!

A spirituality which values narrative

The Zen master Nan-in had a visitor who came to enquire about
the spiritual life. But instead of listening, the visitor kept on
talking about his own ideas. After a while Nan-in served tea. He
poured the tea into the visitor's cup until it was full. Then he
carried on pouring, the tea overflowing on to the table and then
the floor. Finally the visitor could restrain himself no longer.
'Don't you see it's full?' he said. 'You can't get any more in!' 'Just
so,' replied Nan-in, stopping at last. 'And like this cup you too are
full – with your own ideas. How can you expect me to give you
Zen unless you offer an empty cup?'

We could have used this story to make the previous point about
humility in spirituality. If we are so full of our own competence we
can receive neither from God nor from other people. The further
point to make now, however, is that narrative itself has a unique
power to communicate to the heart. It gains this from the importance of the narrative flow in which we all live and by which we
largely define ourselves. It is sets of stories which give identity to
nations, communities, families, churches and individuals – stories
which are told and retold, passed on to children, remembered at
anniversaries, recounted to strangers. And these stories often
carry our deepest beliefs and values; these are the myths by which
we order our lives.

It is not surprising, therefore, that any spirituality which seeks
to be in touch with the deepest realities by which we and others
live will be drawn to narrative, metaphor and poetry. Stories are
evocative and open-ended; they engage the listener; they make
him ask and answer questions. Stories are mischievous, they hint
and subvert; they go to the heart of an issue but give you space to
back off. Stories are cheeky and memorable; they catch you off
guard and slip in when you aren't watching. Moreover, stories
travel light; they don't need textbooks, and people enjoy them. All
of which seems to have been well known to Jesus.

The literature on narrative and faith is rapidly expanding. Stories have long been associated with Jewish spirituality and some forms of Eastern faiths,[13] but the wealth of Christian narrative is vast and rewarding. The Bible is of course packed with it, and the Gospels use narrative as their primary genre. Stories of the desert fathers and the saints have fed the Church for centuries. Narratives of the present century, full of suffering and discovery, are more plentiful than ever; and all the time we are writing our own 'fifth Gospel', the experiences we have of God at work in and around and in spite of us.

Charles Elliott has demonstrated the effectiveness of story in feeding a political spirituality.[14] Many thousands of people have been delighted and inspired by Anthony de Mello's use of stories from the East, and Kathy Galloway has shown the value of giving contemporary clothing to familiar biblical narratives.[15] Narrative has become a key category in much recent thinking about preaching, most of it in the United States.[16] Trevor Dennis and Walter Wangerin on different sides of the Atlantic have been revealing the potential of short stylized fiction to speak to the heart,[17] following the rich tradition of longer, classic works by C.S. Lewis, Charles Williams and J.R.R. Tolkien. A spirituality which uses stories will never be short of material.

A spirituality which is corporate

Excessive individualism may rob a person of personal confidence and political power. It may also rob a person of spiritual identity. The reason for this is both psychological and theological. On the one hand, the individual struggle to make the Christian journey alone can result in frustration and loneliness; on the other hand, the Bible knows no such thing as a solo Christian. The people of God exist together in covenant with Yahweh; the New Testament pictures of the people of the new covenant are nearly always cast in plural form – the spiritual house made of living stones (1 Pet. 2.5), the body made of many members (1 Cor. 12.12). To be a Christian is to have a corporate spiritual identity with the extraordinary rainbow people of God, locally, nationally, internationally, and indeed cosmically, in the communion of saints.

What this means in practice is a commitment to work and worship with the people of God in the Church, even when the cost is high. An ordinand with a strong conviction about the social dimension of the Kingdom of God was a member of a struggling inner-city church. The predominant theology was world-denying; the spirituality was quietist; the political philosophy was conservative. Even his confidence in the case for ordaining women to the priesthood was resisted by most church members. Nevertheless he was committed to the local body of believers, he never stopped caring for the welfare of both church and community and he refused to be in any way embittered or despairing. This was his community, the gift of God, and his privilege and responsibility was to love and enjoy God and to be part of the coming Kingdom in that place.

A corporate spirituality is likely to focus on the Eucharist, where God's people are 'ransomed, healed, restored, forgiven'. It is here that the rumour is confirmed and celebrated that the blind are receiving their sight and the poor are hearing the Good News. It is here that the holy community gather together to receive holy communion and have a foretaste of the holy Kingdom that God intends for us all. None of this can be done alone and none should dare to enter the conflict for the Kingdom in society at large without the sure fellowship of the Body of Christ.

Of course, conflict is endemic to humankind. It is often encountered in the Church before it is encountered in society. However, the evidence of Christian history is that the cross stands as a perpetual symbol of the sad fact that both Church and society resist the values of the Kingdom, and that consequently the Kingdom will come much more through crisis and conflict than through gentle progress. The cross is not a religious luxury but a human necessity. It follows that if they are to bear witness to such a costly path the people of the cross need each other in common cause and loving prayer. Christians therefore need the support and encouragement of their church, home group, prayer cell, or the strength of their membership of the Franciscan Tertiaries, the Iona Community or the Taizé network. Only a corporate spirituality can sustain the transforming vision of the Kingdom of God.

A spirituality which is mission-focused and ecumenical

Some forms of spirituality today are marked by an excess of inwardness. They tend towards escape, and the development of one's own spiritual palate. The temptation is perennial, but it must be resisted, because our life in God is never an end in itself.

Prayer is for a purpose which transcends both domesticity in the Church and self-absorption in the individual. It is to undergird the whole mission of the Church to the whole of the world with the whole of the gospel.

That mission is shaped by identifying what God is doing in the world and joining him in it. It will involve evangelism, social action and the renewal of the Church, and cannot be reduced simply to the collection of more and more Christians. It will be best understood as participating in the renewal of creation, an enterprise so awesome it can only belong to God, but which has to be achieved in human terms by critical attention to detail. The world as we have it can only be a brilliant first sketch of the new creation that will finally be revealed, but that is no reason not to work with all our energy under the One who himself holds the plans of the coming Kingdom.

The spirituality which supports this vision has to be fundamentally mission-orientated. There will be no narrow guarding of 'my' precious prayer life, because prayer and action, sacred and secular, intercession and evangelism – all of these false divisions dissolve in the white heat of the Church's mission. The inwardness of prayer will be greatly needed, but its purpose will be to strengthen the heart for service of the Kingdom of God. Contemplation will indeed be for God's sake, but that God is the bringer of a Kingdom which includes both comfort and discomfort, peace and a sword.

'Better together' is only a slogan, but sometimes a slogan encapsulates an important truth. It is better to work and pray for the Church's mission together, across the churches, than to do it in splendid isolation or spurious purity. The enrichment of ecumenical prayer, however, is not found in bland, inoffensive worship but in the riches and distinctiveness of the traditions. There are times when ecumenical sensibilities require that no particular liturgical rite prevails. However, great benefit is also found by entering as fully as possible into the character and riches of one particular denominational practice and experiencing the insights of that tradition through its own integrity.

At the heart of the contemporary convergence of the churches there is a rethinking of theological shibboleths and a growing weight of experience of shared prayer, study and mission. There has also been the common ownership of a new store of Christian music, and the rediscovery of different forms of prayer which have previously been thought the preserve of particular traditions. An ecumenical spirituality recognizes that God is always bigger than our greatest expectations, always richer than our wildest dreams, and always about to surprise us.

A spirituality of celebration

The challenge of Nietzsche that the disciples of Christ 'should look more redeemed' is a standing challenge to the Christian community. The Jewish Talmud declares that in the day of judgement we will be called to account for every good thing we did not enjoy. The believer is called to celebrate God's goodness in a thousand daily miracles and in the blessed moments when people choose life rather than death. Moreover, Christian joy is not a carefree naivety which hasn't understood the problem, but the deep joy of adults who have faced the pain and found the resurrection. 'Not a euphoric bliss,' wrote Brother Roger of Taizé, 'but that jubilation which comes straight from the wellsprings of eternity.'[18]

It is likely, therefore, that those who are committed to the transformation of lives and of society through the dynamic of loving service will be sustained by a lived experience of resurrection which has come about through hard work and not a little suffering. Those who are most involved in life's hard places often have an inner core of celebration which they have discovered through their Good Friday experiences and without which they would simply not have survived. They have found for themselves how important it is not to let the sorrows of the world make us forget the joy of Christ risen. This joy is infectious; it is good to be around the holy fool who laughs.

At its simplest, Christianity is the life, death and resurrection of Jesus, going on daily in the heart of individuals, the Church and society. The people of God are asked to participate in that divine life, and to share the struggle for renewed lives and a just society. To do this, Christian people need the mental resources of something like the pastoral cycle, and the spiritual resources of a life 'hidden with Christ in God' (Col. 3.3).

Notes

1   Stanley Hauerwas draws attention to the way that communities acquire particular characteristics as they are formed by the stories they habitually retell. See especially *A Community of Character* (University of Notre Dame 1981).

2   Sheppard, D., *Bias to the Poor* (Hodder and Stoughton 1983); Elliott, C., *Praying the Kingdom* (Darton, Longman and Todd 1985); Hughes, G., *God of Surprises* (Darton, Longman and Todd 1985); Wallis, J., *Faithworks: Lessons on Spirituality and Social Action* (SPCK 2002).

3   A good way in to liberation methods of using the Bible is found in Rowland, C. and Corner, M., *Liberating Exegesis; the Challenge of Liberation Theology to Biblical Studies* (SPCK 1990).

4   See for example Davies, J. and Vincent, J., *Mark at Work* (BRF 1986); Fraser, I., *Reinventing Theology as the People's Work* (Wild Goose 1988).

5   Leech, K., *We Preach Christ Crucified* (Darton, Longman and Todd 1994), p. 53.

6   See note 2.

7   Volf, Miroslav, *Exclusion and Embrace* (Abingdon 1996).

8   Green, L., *Let's Do Theology* (Mowbray 1990), p. 144.

9   Many books are available explaining the basic principles of these approaches: e.g. Goldsmith, M. and Wharton, M., *Knowing Me Knowing You* (SPCK 1993); Riso, D., *Personality Types* (The Aquarian Press 1988). Greater value still is gained by attending workshops which use the methods.

10 This process is well explored in Woodhouse, P.W., *In Search of the Kingdom* (Marshall Pickering 1989).

11 Tillich, P., *The Shaking of the Foundations* (Penguin 1962), p. 163.

12 Fraser, op. cit. See also Astley, Jeff, *Ordinary Theology* (Ashgate 2002).

13 The Eastern tradition of stories for Christian spirituality by: de Mello, A., *Sadhana* (Image 1984) and *The Song of the Bird* (Image 1984).

14 Elliott, op. cit., especially chapters 4 and 5.

15 Galloway, K., *Imagining the Gospels* (SPCK 1988). For a useful summary see Stevenson, Peter K., 'Preaching and Narrative' in Day, D., Astley, J. and Francis, L. (eds), *A Reader on Preaching* (Ashgate 2005).

16 For example: Lowry, E., *The Homiletical Plot: the sermon as narrative art form* (Abingdon 1980) and *Doing Time in the Pulpit* (Abingdon 1985).

17 For example: Dennis, T., *Speaking of God* (Triangle 1992); Wangerin, W., *The Manger is Empty* (Spire 1988).

18 Brother Roger, *Itinerary for a Creation in Common* (Taizé).

Appendix A

Community profile

1. Name of area _____

2. What is the total population? _____

3. Are particular age groups dominant? If so, which?

   _____

4. To which socio-economic groups does the working population belong?

   Give approx % in each case

   - professional and managerial _____

   - skilled _____

   - non-manual _____

   - semi-skilled _____

   - unskilled _____

5. What is the local level of unemployment? _____

6. What are the proportions of housing-types in the area?

   - privately owned post-1919 _____

   - privately owned pre-1919 _____

   - privately rented _____

   - council _____

   - housing association _____

7. How many people are there in the average household?

_____

8. On average how often do people move?

_____

9. How many rooms (excluding kitchens and bathrooms) in the main types of house?

_____

10. How many cars are there per household?

_____

11. What proportion of extended families are there?

_____

12. What proportion of school leavers go on to higher education?

_____

13. Neighbourhood relations: how and where do people meet in the area?

_____

_____

14. Are there any particular tensions in the community?

_____

_____

15. What common interest groups are there in the area?

_____

_____

16. Are there any special social problems?

_____

_____

17. Are any major developments planned in the community? Enclose a copy of a Local Plan if one exists.

_____

_____

18. How do people outside the church tend to regard the church?

_____

_____

19. Enclose a map of the area (which may need to be a sketch map for clarity), which shows the main features of the area: roads, types of housing, open space, recreational facilities, schools, pubs, industry, churches, etc.

Appendix B

Church profile (adapt to own tradition)

1. Name of church _____

2. Give figures for church membership/electoral roll (Anglican) for the following years (if available):

   - 1955 _____
   - 1965 _____
   - 1975 _____
   - 1985 _____
   - 1995 _____
   - Present _____

3. What proportion of the membership roll are active members?

   _____

4. (Anglican) What proportion of the electoral roll live in the parish?

   _____

5. What is the approximate socio-economic profile of the membership roll, bearing in mind the conventional divisions?

   - professional and managerial _____
   - foremen and skilled _____
   - non-manual _____
   - semi-skilled _____
   - unskilled _____

- housewives _____
- unemployed _____

6. In church attenders, what is the approximate age
   distribution?

   _____

7. Have there been any recent trends in church membership
   (e.g. growth in young families, decline in youth organizations, greater proportion from outside the area)?

   _____

   _____

8. Enclose a list of church organizations and any special
   features about them (separate sheet).

9. What other important structures are there in church life
   (e.g. leadership team, pastoral care groups, house groups, lay
   training programme, etc)?

   _____

   _____

10. How does leadership operate in the church?

    _____

    _____

11. What are the church's objectives in mission?

    _____

    _____

12. What other churches are there in the area? How does this
    church relate to them?

    _____

    _____

13. Note down any significant events in the 'church story',
    i.e. turning points, crises, major developments.

    _____

    _____

14. What makes this church tick, i.e. what is its real heart, moti-
    vation, controlling vision?

    _____

    _____

Appendix C

Significant event account

A 'significant event' in this context is an event in which you were involved and for which you had some responsibility, which caused you anxiety, bewilderment, hard thinking or pleasure. Give brief answers to the following:

1. Context: give sufficient background to the event for it to be understandable.

   _____

   _____

   _____

   _____

2. Description: describe what happened and how you were feeling about it at the time.

   _____

   _____

   _____

   _____

3. Analysis:

   (a) Personal reflection: why do you think you felt as you
did? and others as they did?

_____

_____

_____

_____

   (b) Social reflection: what other social and structural factors
were involved, if any? i.e. what wider concerns and issues
were actually present, though not articulated?

_____

_____

_____

_____

   (c) Theological reflection: what theological issues were at
stake? what passages of Scripture or what doctrines help
you to make sense of the event now?

_____

_____

_____

_____

4. Evaluation: assess how you handled the event or reacted to
it. What do you learn from it, and what decisions do you
need to make about your future action in similar or other
situations?

_____

_____

_____

_____

Appendix D

Personal reaction sketch

1. What was your initial impression of the church?

   _____

   _____

   _____

2. What have you found most enjoyable?

   _____

   _____

   _____

3. What have you found most difficult?

   _____

   _____

   _____

4. What are the rewards of ministry in the church?

   _____

   _____

   _____

5. What are the frustrations of ministry in the church?

   _____

   _____

   _____

6. What are the main things you have learnt through this
   placement?

   _____

   _____

   _____

7. What has encouraged you about your own gifts and skills?

   _____

   _____

   _____

8. What have you learnt about your own limitations?

   _____

   _____

   _____

9. Is there any action you propose to take as a result of the
   placement?

   _____

   _____

   _____

Appendix E

Sermon evaluation

Preacher: _____

Church: _____

Date: _____

Type of service: _____

Text or subject: _____

Sermon content

1. What do you think was the aim of the sermon?

   _____

   _____

2. How well was the text or subject explained?

   _____

3. Where was 'Good News' to be found in the sermon?

   _____

4. How well was the sermon related to everyday life and
   practical issues? At what points?

   _____

   _____

5. Was your mind informed? Were your emotions touched?
   Was your will challenged?

   _____

   _____

6. How well did the sermon fit into the act of worship as a
whole?

_____

Delivery

1. Were the opening and closing prayers, if any, suitable?

_____

2. How well did the preacher gain your attention at the start?

_____

3. Did you sense a structure or direction in the sermon?

_____

4. How well was the sermon illustrated?

_____

5. Did you ever 'drift off'? Why?

_____

6. Were the language and ideas appropriate to the type of
congregation?

_____

7. Was the preacher audible?

_____

8. Did anything help or distract you in voice, eye contact,
movements, dress, etc.?

_____

9. How well did the preacher end the sermon?

_____

10. What one thing would you encourage the preacher to keep
doing?

_____

_____

11. What one thing would you encourage the preacher to
change?

_____

_____

Bibliography

In this bibliography a range of illustrative and key texts is identified for most chapters. Some books will be valuable for the discussion contained in several of the chapters but they are usually referred to once and not mentioned repeatedly.

Part I

Chapter 2: Practical theology as an academic discipline

Pattison, Stephen, *A Critique of Pastoral Care* (SCM 2000), offers a general survey of the development of pastoral theology alongside some valuable particular insights.

Browning, Don, *A Fundamental Practical Theology* (Fortress 1991) argues for an approach similar to the one outlined here but out of the American scene.

Ballard, Paul H. (ed.), *The Foundations of Pastoral Studies and Practical Theology* (University College, Cardiff 1986), represents a first attempt to draw together the British story.

Campbell, Alastair, *Rediscovering Pastoral Care* (Darton, Longman and Todd 1981), is a British classic, expressing the desire to reinject theology into pastoral action.

Ven, Johannes van der, *Practical Theology* (Kok Pharos 1992) represents the Catholic religious sociology tradition.

Carr, Wesley, *Handbook of Pastoral Studies* (SPCK 1997).

Elford, R. John, *The Pastoral Nature of Theology – An Upholding Presence* (Cassell 1999), arguing all theology is practical.

Wright, Frank, *Pastoral Care Revisited* (SCM 1996).

Forrester, Duncan B., *Truthful Action* (T&T Clark 2000).

Lartey, Emmanuel, *Groundwork of Pastoral Theology* (Epworth 2005).

Ven, Johannes van der, *Ecclesiology in Context* (Eerdmans 1996), from the point of view of empirical theology.

Rahner, Karl, *Theology of Pastoral Action* (Burns and Oates 1968).
Dulles, Avery, *The Craft of Theology* (Gill and Macmillan 1992). Rahner and Dulles represent modern Catholic thinking.
Allan, Joseph J., *The Ministry of the Church – The Image of Pastoral Care* (St Vladimir's Press 1986): an Orthodox reflection.

Chapter 3: The practical theologian

There is a long and abundant literature on ministry. Here, however, we are primarily interested in the minister as the representative theological figure, the one who enables the whole people of God to express their calling in and for the world. This is a selected cross-section of different creative approaches to the theme.

De Gruchy, John, *Theology and Ministry in Context and Crisis* (Harper and Row 1966). An exciting book from a leading South African theologian.
Neuhaus, Richard, *Freedom for Ministry* (Eerdmans 1992).
Holmes, U.T., *The Priest in Community* (Seabury 1978). The last of a trio of books exploring ministry and presence by a leading American Episcopalian who tragically died in mid-career.
Poling, James and Miller, Donald E, *Foundations for a Practical Theology of Ministry* (Abingdon 1985).
Moody, Christopher, *Eccentric Ministry* (Darton, Longman and Todd 1992).
Carr, Wesley, *The Pastor as Theologian* (SPCK 1989).
Tidball, Derek, *Skilful Shepherds* (IVP 1997).
James, M.M. and Francis, Leslie, *Tentmaking* (Gracewing 1998), on the rise of non-stipendiary ministry.
Croft, Stephen, *Ministry in Three Dimensions* (Darton, Longman and Todd 1999).
Bowden, Andrew and West, Michael, *Dynamic Local Ministry* (Continuum 2000).
Gibbs, E. and Coffey, D., *Church Next – Quantum Changes in Christian Ministry* (IVP 2001).
Louden, Stephen H. and Francis, Leslie, *The Naked Parish Priest* (Continuum 2003), studies in the contemporary experience of catholic priests.
Ven, Johannes van der, *Education for Reflective Ministry* (Peeters Hadleigh 1999), a Dutch Catholic perspective.

Chapter 5: Models for practical theology

In this chapter, bibliographical details are found at the end of each section, as the various models of practical theology are introduced.

Part II

Chapter 6: Tools for practical theology

The use of the pastoral cycle is widespread but introductions are not so frequently found.

Green, Laurie, *Power to the Powerless* (Marshall Pickering 1987) describes a particular parochial situation.
Green, L., *Let's Do Theology* (Mowbray 1990) is an accessible guide.

See also some of the liberationist literature indicated in Chapter 5, e.g. Pattison, Stephen, *Pastoral Care and Liberation Theology* (CUP 1994).

Chapter 7: Learning from experience

Green, L., *Let's Do Theology* (Mowbray 1990). This is a basic text for Part II of this book.
Ballard, Paul H. (ed.), *The Foundations of Pastoral Studies and Practical Theology* (University College, Cardiff 1986). Again, a basic text covering many of the issues in practical theology as perceived in the mid 1980s.
Williams, M., *Learning from Experience* (Grove 1981). A brief introduction.
Lovell, G., *Analysis and Design* (Epworth 1995). A valuable book on method in gathering information and understanding in order to work with the community.
Foskett, J., and Lyall, D., *Helping the Helpers*. Covers important aspects of supervised learning on placement.

For local audit see: *Faithworks* (www.faithworks.info).

Chapter 8: Inter-disciplinary working

One of the best ways of ensuring inter-disciplinary competence is to seek out up-to-date surveys of the field of interest. There are two preliminary ways to approach this:

(i) To turn to competent dictionaries or encyclopaedia. It is only possible here to give a small, representative, selection.
(ii) To find up-to-date course text books or other books in that relevant field. Again we can only offer a selection.

This provides a 'jumping off point' for further exploration. Journals also often offer surveys of recent work and keep you up to date through the book reviews.

Dictionaries
Campbell, Alastair V. (ed.), *A Dictionary of Pastoral Care* (SPCK 1987).
Hunter, Rodney (ed.), *Dictionary of Pastoral Care and Counselling* (Abingdon, expanded edition with CD-ROM, 2005).
Atkinson, D. and Field, D. (eds), *New Dictionary of Christian Ethics and Pastoral Theology* (IVP 1995).
Woodward, James and Pattison, Stephen (eds), *Reader in Pastoral and Practical Theology* (Blackwell 2000).
Willows, David and Swinton, John (eds), *Spiritual Dimensions of Pastoral Care* (Jessica Kingsley 2000).
Carr, Wesley (ed.), *The New Dictionary of Pastoral Studies* (SPCK 2002).
Glazier, M. and Hellwig, M.K. (eds), *The Modern Catholic Encyclopedia* (Gill and Macmillan 1994).
Fahlbusch, E. *et al.* (eds), *The Encyclopedia of Christianity* (Eerdmans 2001).
Macquarrie, John and Childress, James (eds), *The New Dictionary of Christian Ethics* (SCM 1986).
Bradshaw, Paul (ed,), *The New Dictionary of Liturgy and Worship* (SCM 2002).
Richardson, A. and Bowden, J. (eds), *A New Dictionary of Christian Theology* (SCM 1989).
Wakefield, Gordon, *A Dictionary of Christian Spirituality* (SCM 1983).
Sutcliffe, John M., *A Dictionary of Religious Education* (SCM 1984).
Bowden, J. (ed.), *Christianity – The Complete Guide* (Continuum 2005).

Psychology and human persons
Browning, Don, *Religious Thought and the Modern Psychologies* (Fortress 1987).
Jacobs, Michael (ed.), *Towards the Fullness of Christ* (Darton, Longman and Todd 1988).
Jacobs, M. (ed.) *Faith or Fear? A Reader in Pastoral Care and Counselling* (Darton, Longman and Todd 1987).
Argyle, Michael, *Psychology and Religion* (Routledge 2000).
Watts, Fraser *et al.*, *Psychology for Christian Ministry* (Routledge 2001).
Watts, Fraser, *Theology and Psychology* (Ashgate 2002).
Fontana, D., *Psychology, Religion and Spirituality* (Blackwell 2003).
Fowler, James, *Faith Development and Pastoral Care* (Fortress 1987).
Slee, Nicola, *Women's Faith Development* (Ashgate 2004).
Adams, Jay E., *More Than Redemption* (Baker Books 1979).

For special concerns see relevant volumes in Library of Pastoral Care (SPCK).

Basic approaches to sociology and sociological method
(i) Introductions to sociological sciences
Bilton, T. *et al.* (eds), *Introductory Sociology* (Palgrave 2002).
Filcher, J. and Scott, J. (eds), *Sociology* (OUP 2003).
Hendry, Jan, *An Introduction to Social Anthropology* (Palgrave 1999).
(ii) Sociology of religion
Davie, Grace, *Religion in Britain Since 1945* (Blackwell 1995).
Davie, Grace, *Religion in Modern Europe* (OUP 2000).
Bruce, Stephen, *Religion in Modern Britain* (OUP 1995).
Parsons, Gerald, *The Growth of Religious Diversity* (Routledge 1993).
Hunt, Stephen J., *Religion in Western Society* (Palgrave 2002).
Woodhead, Linda and Heelas, Paul (eds), *Religion in Modern Times* (Blackwell 2000).
Hamilton, Malcolm, *The Sociology of Religion – Theoretical and Comparative Perspectives* (Routledge 2001).
Zuckerman, Phil, *Invitation to the Sociology of Religion* (Routledge 2003).

Professions and models of ministry
Russell, Anthony, *The Clerical Profession* (SPCK 1980).
Schon, Donald A., *The Reflective Practitioner* (Arena 1999).
Pattison, Stephen, *The Faith of the Managers* (Cassell 1997).
Pattison, Stephen and Pill, Roisin (eds), *Values in Professional Practice* (Radcliffe 2004).
Legood, Giles (ed), *Chaplaincy – The Church's Sector Ministries* (Cassell 1999).
Orchard, Helen, *Hospital Chaplaincy – Modern, Dependable?* (Sheffield Academic Press 2000).
Bowden, Andrew, *Ministry in the Countryside* (Mowbray 1994).
Green, Laurie, *Urban Ministry and the Kingdom of God* (SPCK 2003).

Chapter 9: Theological reflection

Practical examples of theological reflection are found in Green, *Let's Do Theology* and Ballard, *Foundations.*

Taylor, M., *Learning to Care* (SPCK 1983). Outlines a rather cumbersome approach to correlational reflection, but with helpful examples.
Whitehead, J.D. and E.E., *Method in Ministry* (Harper and Row 1980).
Kinast, L. Robert, *Let Ministry Teach – A Guide to Theological Reflection* (Liturgical Press 1996).
O'Connell Killen, P. and Beer J. de, *The Art of Theological Reflection* (Crossroad 2001).
Wells, Sam, *Improvisation: The Drama of Christian Ethics* (SPCK 2004).
Graham, Elaine *et al.* (eds), *Theological Reflection: Methods (vol. I) – Reader (vol. II)* (SCM 2005/06).

For a discussion of the Bible in practical theology:
Ballard, Paul and Holmes, Stephen R. (eds), *The Bible in Pastoral Practice* (Darton, Longman and Todd 2005).

Chapter 10: Mission in context today

Congregational studies
Arbuckle, Gerald A., *Earthing the Gospel* (Chapman 1990).
Gibbs, Eddie, *I Believe in Church Growth* (Hodder and Stoughton 1981).
Hopewell, James F., *Congregation – Stories and Structures* (SCM 1987).
Ammerman, Nancy T. *et al.*, *Studying Congregations* (Abingdon 1998).
Dudley, Carl, *Effective Small Churches in the Twenty-first Century* (Abingdon 2003).
Grundy, Malcolm, *Understanding Congregations* (Mowbrays 1998).
Guest, Mathew *et al.* (eds), *Congregational Studies in the United Kingdom* (Ashgate 2004).
Cameron, H. *et al.*, *Studying Local Churches* (SCM 2005).

Church and community
Henderson, Paul and Thomas, David N., *Skills in Neighbourhood Work* (Routledge 2001).
Twelvetrees, Alan, *Community Work* (Palgrave 2001).
Ballard, Paul (ed.), *Issues in Church Related Community Work* (University College, Cardiff 1990).
Lovell, George, *Analysis and Design* (Epworth 1995).
Lovell, George, *Consultancy, Ministry and Mission* (Burns and Oates 2000).
Furniss, George, *Sociology for Pastoral Care* (SPCK 1995).
Lampard, John S., *Look at Your Church* (Epworth 1975).
Handy, Charles, *Understanding Voluntary Organisations* (Penguin 1988).
Grundy, Malcolm, *Community Work – A Handbook for Volunteer Groups and Local Churches* (Mowbray 1995).
Fineron, Doreen, *Faith in Community Development* (University of Manchester 1993).
Fineron, Doreen *et al.*, *Challenging Communities* (Churches' Community Work Alliance n/d).
Morisy, A. *Beyond the Good Samaritan* (Mowbray 1997).
Morisy, A. *Journeying Out* (Morehouse 2002).

Inter-faith relations
Race, Alan, *Christians and Religious Pluralism – Patterns in the Christian Theology of Religions* (SCM 1983), the classic exposition of the threefold pattern.
Race, Alan, *Inter-faith Encounter* (SCM 2001).
Plantinga, Richard J. (ed.), *Christianity and Plurality – Classic and Contemporary Readings* (Blackwell 1999).

D'Costa, Gavin, *Christian Uniqueness Reconsidered – The Myth of a Pluralistic Theology of Religions* (Orbis 1990).
D'Costa, Gavin, *The Meeting of Religions and the Trinity* (T&T Clark 2000).
Ramachandra, Vinoth, *Faiths in Conflict* (IVP 1999).
Dupuis, Jaques SJ, *Christianity and the Religions – From Confrontation to Dialogue* (Darton, Longman and Todd 2002), a Catholic survey and study.
Hooker, Roger and Lamb, Christopher, *Love the Stranger – Christian Ministry in Multi-faith Areas* (SPCK 1986).
Hooker, Roger and Sargent, John (eds), *Belonging to Britain – Christian Perspectives on Religion and Identity in a Plural Society* (CCBI 1991).
Cracknell, Kenneth, *Towards a New Relationship – Christians and People of Other Faiths* (Epworth 1986).
Trivasse, Keith, *Walking Toward the Mosque* (Contact Pastoral Trust 2004).
Haslam, D. *The Churches and 'Race': A pastoral approach* (Grove Books 2001).

Mission
Abraham, William J. *The Logic of Evangelism* (Hodder and Stoughton 1989).
Avis, Paul, *A Ministry Shaped by Mission* (T&T Clark 2005).
Barrow, Simon and Smith, Graeme (eds), *Christian Mission in Western Society* (Churches Together in Britain and Ireland 2001).
Bosch, David J., *Witness to the World: the Christian Mission in Theological Perspective* (Marshall, Morgan and Scott 1980).
Bosch, David J. *Transforming Mission: Paradigm Shifts in the Theology of Mission* (Orbis 1991).
Donovan, Vincent J., *The Church in the Midst of Creation* (SCM 1989).
Kirk, J. Andrew and Vanhoozer, Kevin J. (eds), *To Stake a Claim: Mission and the Western Crisis of Knowledge* (Orbis 1999).
Kirk, J. Andrew, *What is Mission? Theological Explorations* (Darton, Longman and Todd 1999).
Newbigin, Lesslie, *The Open Secret* (SPCK 1978).
Newbigin, Lesslie, *Gospel in a Pluralist Society* (SPCK 1989).
Stott, John, *Christian Mission in the Modern World* (Falcon 1975).
Taylor, John V. *The Go-Between God: The Holy Spirit and the Christian Mission* (SCM 1972).
Ward, Pete, *Liquid Church* (Paternoster 2002).
Ward, Pete, *Selling Worship* (Paternoster 2005).

Post-modernism
Lyon, David, *Postmodernity* (Open University 1994).
Grenz, Stanley J., *A Primer on Postmodernism* (Eerdmans 1996).

Heelas, Paul, *The New Age Movement* (Blackwell 1996).
Heslam, Peter (ed.), *Globalization and the Good* (SPCK 2004).
Lynch, Gordon, *Understanding Theology and Popular Culture* (Blackwell 2005).
Walker, Andrew, *Telling the Story – Gospel, Mission and Culture* (SPCK 1996).
Goodliff, Paul, *Care in a Confused Climate – Pastoral Care and Postmodern Culture* (Darton, Longman and Todd 1998).

Chapter 11: From reflection to action

Green, *Let's Do Theology*, is particularly valuable here.
Hull, J., *What Prevents Christian Adults from Learning?* (SCM 1985). A thoughtful study of some of the possible outcomes of the reflective process, and what stops them.
Craig,Y., *Learning for Life* (Mowbray 1994). A broad, practical survey of many learning methods, their strengths and weaknesses.
Kane, M., *What Kind of God?* (SCM 1986). Holds together models of reflection and the demands of action.
Fontana, David, *Psychology for Teachers* (Palgrove 1995).
Adair, John and Nelson, John, *Creative Church Leadership* (Canterbury 2004).
Torry, Malcolm, *Managing God's Business* (Ashgate 2006).
Pattison, Stephen, *The Faith of the Managers* (Cassell 1997).

Chapter 12: A spirituality equal to the task

Elliott, C., *Praying the Kingdom* (Darton, Longman and Todd 1985).
Hughes, G., *God of Surprises* (Darton, Longman and Todd 1985). Both these DLT books exemplify the process and the necessity of holding spirituality and action together.
Vanstone,W.H., *Love's Endeavour, Love's Expense* (Darton, Longman and Todd 1977). A classic plea for ministry to be founded in a theology and spirituality of self-emptying.
Leech, K., *Spirituality and Pastoral Care* (Sheldon 1986).
Moody, C., *Eccentric Ministry* (Darton, Longman and Todd 1992).
Neuhaus, R., *Freedom for Ministry* (Eerdmans 1992). A powerful and sustained argument for the authentic Christian roots of ministry.
Wink,W., *Engaging the Powers* (Fortress 1992).
McGrath, A.E., *Christian Spirituality – An Introduction* (Blackwell 1999).
Holmes, U.T., *History of Christian Spirituality – An Analytic Introduction* (Morehouse 2002).
Wakefield, Gordon S., *Groundwork of Christian Spirituality* (Epworth 2001).
Thorne, B., *Person Centred Counselling and Christian Spirituality – The Secular and the Holy* (Whurr 1998).
Volf, Miroslav, *Exclusion and Embrace* (Abingdon 1996).
Astley, Jeff, *Ordinary Theology* (Ashgate 2002).
Wallis, J. *Faithworks: Lessons on Spirituality and Social Action* (SPCK 2002).

Index